MARK CUBAN:

The Maverick Billionaire

By Sean Huff

KEEN PUBLISHING
Jacksonville, FL

The Modern Moguls Series

Entrepreneur, media mogul, celebrity and the ultimate sports fan... Mark Cuban is one of the most colorful and controversial billionaires of our time. A self-made man who has inspired millions to follow their own dreams.

"Mark Cuban: The Maverick Billionaire" is the first in the Modern Moguls series of biographical profiles, spotlighting the men and women who shape our modern business landscape.

Table of Contents

Chapter 1: The Maverick

Mark Cuban sits in one of the most high-profile chairs in entertainment. He's comfortable. Exactly where he wants to be.

A few hundred people in the room have their eyes affixed on him. Several cameras record his five minute interview, which will later be beamed to millions of TV viewers. On either side of him sit two A-list celebrities paying him their undivided attention.

This is Mark Cuban, the energetic, passionate technology genius who turned two companies into billions of dollars of personal wealth before he became a household name when he acquired the NBA's Dallas Mavericks.

With all the topics this interviewer could quiz Cuban about, he chooses to lead off the chat with a question about a disgraced baseball player and the leadership of Major League Baseball, a sport in which Cuban has no financial interest or presence.

Without understanding Mark Cuban, one might even wonder if he belonged on *The Tonight Show* in the first place. He was originally scheduled to appear two days before this particular Thursday night in August of 2013, but he was bumped by President Barack Obama.

To reschedule his appearance, Cuban had to rearrange his schedule, one that is jammed full, given the mogul's many business interests. And people will usually only subject themselves to late-night talk shows to shill for their movies, books or TV shows, none of which Cuban had to talk up on that program.

So why would *Tonight Show* host Jay Leno begin his interview with a basketball team owner by asking for his thoughts on how Major League Baseball handled superstar Alex Rodriguez's alleged use of performance enhancing drugs?

Because Mark Cuban has strong opinions on almost everything and he will express them without filter, seemingly regardless of the consequences. And sitting next to actor Robin Williams, the first guest on that episode, Cuban did not disappoint.

When Leno asked about Rodriguez's 200+ game ban for using performance enhancing drugs, Cuban accused MLB Commissioner Bud Selig of waging a personal vendetta and not following the league's own rules on handling drug violations.

"Horrible. I think it's disgraceful what Major League Baseball is trying to do to him. It's not that he doesn't deserve to be suspended, he does," Cuban said. "But they have policies in place. First-time offenders, 50 games. Second time, 100... 214 games? That's personal. And I got to tell you, my experiences with Major League Baseball -- and after all this there's no chance I'm going to be able to buy a team -- it's basically become Bud Selig's mafia. He runs it the way he wants to run it."

He went on to accuse the league of doing "everything possible" to keep him from buying the Texas Rangers in 2010.

"They had lawyers in there trying to change the rules, they had people trying to put up more money. It was horrible," the billionaire blasted.[1]

Cuban's words appeared in hundreds if not thousands of blogs, news reports and sports columns the next day. Whether he intended to or not, Mark Cuban received a whole lot of publicity.

And if you think he only expresses opinions when there's little risk of punishment or consequences, you don't know Mark Cuban.

---

[1] "Mark Cuban Rips Bud Selig on A-Rod Suspension on Tonight Show." Huffington Post, August 9, 2013. Retrieved from http://www.huffingtonpost.com/2013/08/09/mark-cuban-bud-selig-a-rod-suspension_n_3731984.html

Look up the word 'maverick' in the dictionary, and the definitions fit Cuban in nearly every respect. The only thing missing is the mogul's photo next to the entry.

A maverick is defined as "a lone dissenter, as an intellectual, an artist, or a politician, who takes an independent stand apart from his or her associates." It can also refer to "a person pursuing rebellious, even potentially disruptive, policies or ideas."

Some of the synonyms provided for maverick include nonconformist, individualist, free thinker, loner, rebel, and loose cannon. Aside from loner, all of those labels surely apply to one Mark Cuban.

The "lone dissenter" aspect of being a maverick is something that Cuban considers good business practice.

"Wherever I see people doing something the way it's always been done, the way it's 'supposed' to be done, following the same old trends, well, that's just a big red flag to me to go look somewhere else. When you've got 10,000 people trying to do the same thing, why would you want to be number 10,001?"[2]

---

[2] What I've Learned: Mark Cuban. Esquire.com, November 17, 2008. Retrieved from http://www.esquire.com/features/what-ive-learned/ESQ1206BBCUBAN_182_1

Being rebellious and disruptive supports the Mark Cuban brand. It's an identity that has become known in multiple circles for eschewing authority, challenging the status quo, and speaking "truth to power" in almost every institution.

Those traits are often portrayed negatively, but Cuban has created a persona that would make a worthy protagonist in a best-selling novel. What makes Cuban a likable figure is that the persona is genuine.

He's the same person no matter the setting. One would be hard-pressed to find any hypocrisy in his myriad volumes of blogs and quotes. Cuban is a rarity in today's society: an anti-establishment billionaire. Over the years he has criticized many of the institutions that people hold sacred.

Mark Cuban would probably say the reason he is wealthy is because he's always stood on the opposite side of the elite. Even though he now has money, he's not about to join them.
That includes his fellow owners in the National Basketball Association.

While his peers act the part of dignified team owner, Cuban acts more like his customers, the fans. And if there's one downside to owning the Dallas Maverick for Mark Cuban, it's that he has somebody to whom he has to answer.

No, David Stern is not his boss. But the commissioner of the National Basketball Association and the league he has presided over for 30 years has rules. And Cuban frequently breaks those edicts, especially ones that forbid public criticism of the league's referees, to the tune of several million dollars in his dozen years of team ownership.

Following a meltdown during the 2006 NBA Finals that cost Cuban a $250,000 fine (See chapter titled, "The Rooter"), the league's owners passed a set of rules loosely referred to as the "Cuban rules of conduct." Among the new stipulations was a ban on owners venturing onto the court during games. During a meeting among league officials and owners regarding the new statutes, Cuban walked out before the vote of the owners. "I was pissed that, of all the things the league needed to pay attention to, this was on the top of their list," he said. "It showed how political the league is. But I'm well past that."[3]

Stern said part of the justification for the rules was to prevent owners from overshadowing the games.

---

[3] Leonard, D. (2007). MARK CUBAN MAY BE A BILLIONAIRE, BUT WHAT HE REALLY NEEDS IS RESPECT. Fortune, 156(8), 172-182.

Therein lies one of many differences between the two adversaries. Cuban's brand is about being in the spotlight. He may not want to completely dominate the game action, but he does want to be a part of it. His anarchistic ways support his personal brand and are part of what makes him a fan favorite. They are also the antithesis of Stern's desire to have law and order in his league, especially amongst the ownership group. He is about structure and control, and part of maintaining control is structuring the league in a way that owners stay in the background.

While the two have had many differences and exchanges of fine payments over the years, Cuban does have respect for Stern as a visionary. When asked about the commissioner's legacy as he prepares to leave the office after 30 years, Cuban replied: "I think it's one of a focus on growth and recognizing that the NBA is in the entertainment business and that it's a global product, not just a local product. Whatever platforms that took us to, he was ready to go. He wasn't protective at all. He was wide open. I think that was great."[4]

Perhaps Cuban and Stern aren't so different after all.

---

[4] Mark Cuban Teases David Stern. ESPN.com, October 26, 2012. Retrieved from http://espn.go.com/dallas/nba/story/_/id/8556905/dallas-mavericks-mark-cuban-jokes-save-money-fines-david-stern-gone

Neither, for that matter, are he and Donald Trump, who has also drawn Cuban's ire on several occasions.

The feud between the two billionaire celebrities began in 2004 when Cuban hosted *The Benefactor*, a short-lived reality-based program in which Cuban would give a $1 million prize to the contestant that demonstrated the skills Cuban deemed necessary to be successful.

Many, including Trump, thought the show was a copy-cat of *The Apprentice*, which had debuted months before. The cancellation of *The Benefactor* prompted Trump to write a slap-in-the-face letter to Cuban. Cuban kept it for almost a decade, then read it aloud during a March 2013 episode of *The Tonight Show* (an earlier appearance than the one in which he criticized Major League Baseball).

Trump's letter read:

> "I am truly sorry to hear that your show has been canceled for lack of ratings. When I initially called you to congratulate you on The Benefactor -- little did you or I realize how disastrous and embarrassing it would turn out to be for you. If you ever decide to do another show, please call me and I will be happy to lend a helping hand."

That fanned the flames of a Twitter war between the two that had been brewing for several months. In November 2012, Cuban offered Trump $1 million to shave his head shortly after the latter publicly offered President Barack Obama $5 million to produce a birth certificate that would prove he's an American citizen.

Following Cuban's *Tonight Show* jab, Trump responded with a series of tweets critical of his rival, 17 in less than a week, including:

> "**@mcuban** has less TV persona than any other person I can think of. He's an arrogant, crude, dope who met some very stupid people."

> "why does **@mcuban** continue to embarrass the 31-35 & 11th place **@dallasmavs** with childish behavior."

When a follower asked Trump "what's the best confidence builder," Trump responded that it was "going against losers like Mark Cuban!"

Cuban, of course, responded: "You just see this crazy life I have & you're in awe. I'm just gonna take over the world while you getting mad." [5]

Cuban also makes his beefs with former Mavericks players and opposing team members public. In 2012, Cuban thought he had an agreement with veteran point guard Jason Kidd, believing he would retire from the franchise. Instead, Kidd signed a free agent deal with the New York Knicks.

Cuban publicly expressed his discontent over Kidd's decision:

> "I thought he (Kidd) was coming (back). I was pissed. J-Kidd's a big boy, he can do whatever he wants. But you don't change your mind like that. I'm sure I'll get over it at some point, but as of right now, I wouldn't put J-Kidd's number in the rafters." [6]

---

[5] Twitter Wars: Donald Trump vs Mark Cuban. Yahoo.com, March 19, 2013. Retrieved from http://sports.yahoo.com/blogs/nba-ball-dont-lie/twitter-wars-donald-trump-vs-mark-cuban-183542949--nba.html

[6] Mark Cuban Won't Retire Jason Kidd's Jersey Because He Went to the Knicks. Yahoo.com, August 21, 2012. Retrieved from http://sports.yahoo.com/blogs/nba-ball-dont-lie/mark-cuban-won-t-retire-jason-kidd-jersey-223414404--nba.html

One of Cuban's most infamous run-ins with a player occurred in 2009. After a Mavericks game with the Denver Nuggets in Denver, in which Dallas lost on a last-second three-pointer, Cuban reportedly confronted the mother of then-Nuggets forward Kenyon Martin and called her son a "thug" and a "punk." Cuban was reportedly upset about Martin's physical style of play during the game. Cuban later apologized on his blog. [7]

Cuban doesn't limit his sharp tongue to matters of basketball. He is a journalist's dream source in that he will dispense his opinion on just about any topic he follows, without a single thought about filtering himself for political correctness. He doesn't even need to be asked a question; through his blog and Twitter feed, he will volunteer his beliefs. And no matter whether it's his own writing or an article by somebody else, Cuban almost never offers an opinion without a heavy dose of expletives and sarcasm.

Mark Cuban on the stock market: "Wall Street has done an AMAZING job of creating conventional wisdom. 'Buy and Hold' is the 2nd most misleading marketing slogan ever, after the brilliant 'rinse and repeat' message on every shampoo bottle. We as a

---

[7] Report: Cuban called Martin a 'Thug'. ESPN.com, May 11, 2009. Retrieved from http://sports.espn.go.com/nba/playoffs/2009/news/story?id=4157481

country have fallen for it. Every message from every marketer of stocks tell us: Young or old, if you can hold for the long term, things will work out for you. That is total bullshit. It's for suckers." [8]

Mark Cuban on large publicly traded corporations: "I'm not against government involvement in times of need. I am for recognizing that big public companies will continue to cut jobs in an effort to prop up stock prices, which in turn stimulates the need for more government involvement." [9]

Mark Cuban on the merits of earning an MBA degree: "I think an MBA is an absolute waste of money. If you have a hole in your knowledge base, there are a ton of online courses you can take. I don't give any advantage to someone in hiring because they have an MBA." [10]

---

[8] The Stock Market is for Suckers... Blog Maverick, January 3, 2006. Retrieved from
http://blogmaverick.com/2006/01/03/the-stock-market-is-for-suckers/
[9] The Most Patriotic Thing You Can Do. Blog Maverick, September 19, 2011. Retrieved from
http://blogmaverick.com/2011/09/19/the-most-patriotic-thing-you-can-do-2/
[10] Mark Cuban: What Entrepreneurs Need to Know Before Starting a Business. Entrepreneur.com, December 26, 2012. Retrieved from
http://www.entrepreneur.com/blog/225357

Another institution Cuban has expressed contempt for is politics. He rarely makes contributions to political campaigns or organizations, despite having more than enough money to do so. He summed up his sentiments about the way politicians try to fix the economy in a blog post during the 2008 presidential campaign:

> "The cure to our economic problems is the Entrepreneurial Spirit of All Americans. Instead of bitching at each other, could one Presidential candidate please show even the least bit of leadership and character and stand up for and encourage the entrepreneurs in this country?
>
> I don't care who is friends with whom, who preached when you went to church, whether you know the actual role of the Vice President, whether you voted with President Bush. I don't care about any of the mudslinging going back and forth. All it does is waste the time of every potential voter. All of that is meaningless.
>
> What we need is our candidates to stop yelling at each other and start looking at the American people and encouraging the best of who we are. That is who I want to get behind.

That is what I would like to see for our country." [11]

Several of Cuban's most recent business ventures revolve around investigative journalism. He started a non-profit foundation that funds three websites designed to expose the malfeasance of government and corporations.

ShareSleuth.com investigates and reports on white collar fraud and other abuses of capitalism, while BailoutSleuth.com "tracks the flow of taxpayer money from the Troubled Asset Relief Program and other federal economic stability initiatives, with an emphasis on transparency and accountability." It also reports on bank failures. The third site, JunketSleuth.com, tracks travel by federal employees, members of Congress and their staffs.

"The websites are because I have a strong distrust for the one percent of government employees who put their careers ahead of doing the right thing," Cuban said. "These efforts were a response to that. If we catch one government crook or provide the information that allows someone else to do so, it will have been worth it. I consider it a small price to pay

---

[11] The Cure to our Economic Problems. Blog Maverick, October 23, 2008. Retrieved from http://blogmaverick.com/2012/09/17/the-cure-to-our-economic-problems-2/

for doing a civic duty. I consider it a patriotic effort. If Share Sleuth continues to discover less-than-savory activity in the business world, it's worth it." [12]

In addition to the websites, his AXS TV network's signature program is *Dan Rather Reports*, which allows the former CBS News anchor to uncover wrongdoing in government and the corporate world. And Cuban's 2929 Productions produced an award winning documentary detailing the Enron scandal, called *The Smartest Guys in the Room*.

Cuban also has contempt for some of his fellow billionaires and upper class citizens who do everything they can to avoid paying taxes and make even more money. He writes that the most patriotic think a person can do is "bust your ass and get rich. Make a boatload of money. Pay your taxes. Lots of taxes. Hire people. Train people. Pay people. Spend money on rent, equipment, services. Pay more taxes. When you make a shitload of money, do something positive with it. If you are smart enough to make it, you will be smart enough to know where to put it to work." [13]

---

[12] Mark Cuban's Business Model. Columbia Journalism Review, February 23, 2011. Retrieved from
http://www.cjr.org/reports/mark_cubans_business_model.php?page=all

[13] The Most Patriotic Thing You Can Do. Blog Maverick, September 19, 2011. Retrieved from

Though he doesn't think tax policy prevents people from becoming successful, he has the opposite to say about the U.S. patent system. But he didn't just write a blog or talk about his disdain for the system on a talk show. In true Cuban fashion, the bombastic billionaire funded an endowed chair at The Electronic Frontier Foundation, a digital civil rights organization. He titled the chair, "The Mark Cuban Chair to Eliminate Stupid Patents."

His issue with the current system: "Dumbass patents are crushing small businesses. I have had multiple small companies I am an investor in have to fight or pay trolls for patents that were patently ridiculous. There is no place for software patents and most tech patents are not original in the first place. They are merely 'remixes' of early technology." [14]

Another institution he would like to dismantle is the NCAA, the governing body of collegiate sports. Cuban was once quoted as saying he wants to buy

---

http://blogmaverick.com/2011/09/19/the-most-patriotic-thing-you-can-do-2/

[14] Mark Cuban's Awesome Justification for Endowing a Chair to 'Eliminate Stupid Patents.' Techcrunch.com, January 31, 2013. Retrieved from http://techcrunch.com/2013/01/31/mark-cubans-awesome-justification-for-endowing-a-chair-for-eliminating-stupid-patents/

four colleges and extract them from the authority of the NCAA. The reason: he thinks college athletes should be paid, and he would personally pay for scholarships and for their services as athletes.

> "If you're in the Journalism School and you get a job working for The Wall Street Journal during spring semester, and you get paid for it, that wouldn't be a bad thing. That would be a grand slam. That would be something everyone would be proud of... And it's the same with everything except athletics... the NCAA doesn't want you to be the best athlete. They want you to be the best amateur athlete.

> So to me, that's just hypocrisy. I can't do it while I own an NBA team. But if I could pull that off, it would be one of the few reasons I would sell the Mavs. Just to be able to shove it up the NCAA's rear..." [15]

Being a maverick is about more than challenging authority and the status quo. Mark Cuban, the maverick, establishes the foundation for his many other identities.

---

[15] 20 Questions for Mark Cuban. Magbloom.com, February/March 2008. Retrieved from http://www.magbloom.com/wp-content/uploads/2012/02/20Q_bloom10.pdf

He is also an architect who has built empires based on his ideas, his drive, and his determination.

He is a visionary who spots the potential of new technology long before the masses.

He is an entertainer who brings unique content to his TV network and movie theater chain.

He is a rooter of all sports, the ultimate fan who will never shed that fandom for the sake of team ownership.

He is an investor who has maximized his wealth and helped others off the ground.

He is a celebrity who never shies from a camera or a spotlight.

And he is a king, not in the royal sense, but in his own world.

His kingdom began in a modest Pittsburgh neighborhood with a stack of garbage bags and a desire for some new shoes.

Chapter 2: The Architect

At the age of 12, Mark Cuban wanted something.

What he desired was a new pair of shoes, Pumas to be exact. His father, while playing cards with his friends, refused. The ones Mark already had were adequate, his father reasoned, adding that he would not provide his son with anything more than his basic needs.

If the young boy wanted more, he would have to earn it.

Cuban learned for the first time that nobody was just going to hand him money or possessions.

During this encounter, one of his father's card-playing buddies jokingly suggested he earn extra money by selling garbage bags in the neighborhood door-to-door. Young Mark Cuban took him seriously, figuring every house needed garbage bags.

He earned enough for his Pumas.

Cuban was born to sell. Once, as a youngster, he accompanied his father to a large stamp collecting show. He bought several stamps on one floor, then turned right around and sold them -- at the same show -- for a profit on another floor. [16]

Nobody gave Mark money for college, so he earned it by selling stamps and coins, starting a chain letter, and giving paid disco lessons. He also, while still in school, managed to purchase a bar near the University of Indiana. To accomplish this he raised money, selling shares of this business to his friends. He lured customers in the door with cheap drinks and wet T-shirt contests, then schmoozed them enough that, as one acquaintance put it: "People came to see him." [17]

In his early career after college, Cuban discovered that jobs came with strings attached. It wasn't just the trade-off between doing a certain amount of work for a certain amount of pay. He discovered quickly that the employee-employer relationship offered little freedom. Back in those days, few of his supervisors would give him the space or the permission to showcase the full breadth of his skills and hard work.

---

[16] Mark Cuban: From Neighborhood VAR to Internet Czar. CRN.com, October 22, 1999. Retrieved from http://www.crn.com/news/channel-programs/18810686/mark-cuban-from-neighborhood-var-to-internet-czar.htm
[17] Leonard, D. (2007). MARK CUBAN MAY BE A BILLIONAIRE, BUT WHAT HE REALLY NEEDS IS RESPECT. Fortune, 156(8), 172-182.

They tried to put Cuban in a box. And when they did, he broke free.

His first escape occurred during his initial job out of college, at Mellon Bank in his hometown of Pittsburgh. Cuban earned a job helping to computerize the bank's electronic files. While many college grads would have been satisfied just having a job during a period of economic recession in 1980, Cuban wanted to be more entrepreneurial. So he sent notes to the CEO with cut-out magazine articles about how the company could save money. He started a group called the Rookie Club made up of the bank's younger employees and would invite senior executives to talk to the bunch. He started a company newsletter.

All of these efforts failed to earn Cuban the praise from his boss he thought he had earned. He received the exact opposite. One day, his supervisor called Cuban into the office and asked him "Who the f--- do you think you are?" When Cuban defended his actions, the boss told him never to go over him again. Cuban left the company shortly after.

He made his way back to Indiana for a brief time before his college friends coaxed him to move to Dallas. They promised abundant jobs and women.

He got a position as a salesperson for Your Business Software, which sold PC software to businesses and consumers, and quickly rose to be one of its top salesman. This was largely due to the hands-on technical skills he developed by reading manuals and studying computer code.

One day, he was scheduled to open up the office, but instead wanted to close a sale with a customer and collect a $15,000 check, a tenth of which Cuban would receive as commission. His boss told him no, but Cuban disobeyed and picked up the check.

He was fired on the spot.

"But being fired from that job was the determining factor in my business life," Cuban wrote. "I decided then and there to start my own company. I didn't have that much to lose, and it was something that I knew I had to do." [18]

What he did have was a Rolodex full of contacts. Working from his apartment, he called those former clients and offered to service their computers with a money-back guarantee. In 1983, he started a company called MicroSolutions using a $500 loan from a client of his sales gig. The company sold

---

[18] Burke, M. (2013). At Age 25 Mark Cuban Learned Lessons About Leadership That Changed His Life. Forbes.Com

software, and also provided training and software configuration.

Cuban wrote his own programs and immersed himself in the industry by studying Microsoft and Lotus. He eventually transitioned the company into developing local area networks, which is when things really took off.

Following their leader, MicroSolutions's employees worked long hours. Cuban offered competitive prices but a level of customer service typically provided only by high-end providers. He studied every new technology that came on the market to an obsessive degree, to ensure he knew more about it than anybody. He became a beta tester and proving ground for innovation.

But technical knowledge was only part of the equation to building a successful enterprise. Cuban understood the power of a strong brand image. While similar companies housed themselves in humble accommodations to limit their overhead expenses, Cuban rented space in the Dallas Infomart, the Taj Mahal of Dallas' high-tech industry. Apple, MCI WorldCom and Xerox had offices there, and Cuban wanted MicroSolutions to appear just as big. [19]

---

[19] Mark Cuban: From Neighborhood VAR to Internet Czar. CRN.com, October 22, 1999. Retrieved from

Cuban read business books and pored over market research as much as computer manuals. The knowledge he acquired kept him one step ahead of his competitors. His competitive spirit drove him to increase that gap. His salesmanship got him invited to industry events reserved for big players, and also helped him find partners to subsidize his rent and marketing initiatives.

Another key to the success of MicroSolutions was its disproportionately high number of salespeople compared to rivals. Cuban wanted more feet on the street so the company could make more calls, knock on more doors and always be ready to respond when opportunity arose.

By the time he sold the firm in 1990 to CompuServe, MicroSolutions was generating $30 million in revenues and employed 85 people.

"I ended up making about $2.2 million," Cuban said. "I bought a lifetime pass on American Airlines and I just started traveling."

http://www.crn.com/news/channel-programs/18810686/mark-cuban-from-neighborhood-var-to-internet-czar.htm

After "retiring" for a few years, the lure of business and competition were too much. Cuban and his college friend Todd Wagner founded AudioNet, which later became Broadcast.com.

Cuban has been interviewed countless times, but anybody who reads his blog posts or approaches the man himself hoping for some instantaneous magic potion for prosperity will be sorely disappointed. Every piece of advice he's ever given boils down to a concept that is simple to explain, but hard for many to execute: Entrepreneurs just have to take the chance and work hard to make it happen.

In his book, *How to Win at the Sport of Business*, Cuban lays out 12 rules for entrepreneurs. The first one is "Don't start a company unless it's an obsession." The second rule is that having an exit strategy demonstrates that your pursuit is not an obsession. In his view, if a business is an obsession, it's not really a risk to go after it because being obsessed means doing all the necessary preparation and leg work to make the company grow. An entrepreneur's obsession means he or she can persuade prospects and make sales, even if they say no a few times.

One of Cuban's favorite expressions is "No Balls, No Baby." He taught this lesson to a friend during the startup phase of MicroSolutions. Cuban and the acquaintance were walking together when Cuban asked him to become a partner in his new business. The friend hemmed and hawed before finally passing on the opportunity. Cuban slapped the man in the face. When asked why, Cuban responded: "That's your wake-up call in life, pal. When opportunity presents itself, you need to be prepared to take it." Cuban never asked again.[20]

> "Most people don't want to cross that line. There's safety on one side, uncertainty on the other. Most people don't take that step. And it's not even so much that they're afraid to take the step; it's that they know deep down that they didn't do the work necessary to be prepared, and that's the big difference. Most people think, 'Oh, I have a great idea, and the only thing missing is that I don't have the connections, I don't have the access to money.' But that's the biggest bunch of bullshit. The minute anyone says that to me, I know they're a failure.
>
> Because if you're prepared and you know what it takes, it's not a risk. You just have to

---

[20] The Billionaire. Esquire.com, April 1, 2000. Retrieved from http://www.esquire.com/features/billionaire-cuban-sound-0400

figure out how to get there. There is always a way to get there." [21]

Another one of Cuban's strongly held beliefs is that entrepreneurs should never finance their startups with debt. "There are so many uncertainties involved with starting a business, yet the one certainty that you have is paying back your loan. And the bank doesn't care about your business." [22]

So how does a company get started? Again, it's about effort. Especially in today's world, capital is not necessary for the large majority of startup companies, he says. Studying some of Cuban's philosophies and reading what his business acquaintances say about him reveals several themes.

First, Cuban believes business owners need to do the work themselves when they're starting out. Entrepreneurs make the mistake of spending too much on things they could do themselves, either because they don't want to work hard enough or

---

[21] What I've Learned: Mark Cuban. Esquire.com, November 17, 2008. Retrieved from http://www.esquire.com/features/what-ive-learned/ESQ1206BBCUBAN_182_1
[22] MARK CUBAN, O. (n.d). MARK CUBAN, OWNER, DALLAS MAVERICKS IS INTERVIEWED ON BLOOMBERG TV REGARDING ENTREPRENEURS. Financial Markets Regulatory Wire, June 13, 2013

because they think too big to begin with. Do your own advertising instead of hiring a marketing firm. Make your own sales calls rather than hiring salespeople. And use your own money instead of borrowing from a bank. As you grow and start to earn money, then you can use those profits to reinvest in your business.

Even as large as it has grown, Cuban believes in keeping his empire as flat as possible. "If you have managers reporting to managers in a startup, you will fail," he wrote in his book. "Once you get beyond startup, if you have managers reporting to managers, you will create politics."

A man who hands out free game systems to his players and free ice cream bars to his office staff nonetheless despises the idea of smaller companies and startups spending on unnecessary items. "A sure sign of failure for a startup is when someone sends me logo-embroidered polo shirts," he writes in the book. "If your people are at shows and in public, it's okay to buy for your own employees, but if you really think people are going to wear your branded polo when they're out and about, you are mistaken and have no idea how to spend your money."

His other rules are fairly simple. Hire people who will love working for you and make sure they're having fun on the job. Know exactly how your company will make sales. Work on building a company, not an empire. "If the person demands to fly first class or to bring over a personal secretary, run away. If an exec won't go on sales calls, run away. They are empire builders and will pollute your company."

He also believes that you can't rely on your customers to tell you want they want. It's your job as the entrepreneur to convince them they want what you're offering.

> "Entrepreneurs need to be reminded that it's not the job of their customers to know what they don't. In other words, your customers have a tough enough time doing their jobs. They don't spend time trying to reinvent their industries or how their jobs are performed. Sure, every now and then you come across an exception. But you can't bet the company on your finding that person among your customers.
>
> Instead, part of every entrepreneur's job is to invent the future. I also call it 'kicking your own ass.' Someone is out there looking to put you out of business. Someone is out there who thinks they have a better idea than you have. A better solution than you have. A better or more efficient product than you have. If there is someone out there who can 'kick your ass'

by doing it better, it's part of your job as the owner of the company to stay ahead of them and 'kick your own ass' before someone else does." [23]

Cuban's love of sports played a part in his entrepreneurial success. He loves to compete and considers business the ultimate sport, whether he's a player or coaching a startup in which he's invested.

As a student at Indiana University, Cuban participated on the school's rugby team. When recently asked about the lessons he learned from the rugged, violent sport that carried over into his business life, Cuban replied: "When it hurts, keep on going. That you can always play a little harder. That there's going to be someone bigger and faster and stronger all the time, and hopefully you can play a little bit smarter. And teamwork counts. When you're in a scrum or in a pack, not always the biggest guys push the scrum the farthest. And not always the biggest guys tackle the hardest. You learn what teamwork means and how to push yourself personally." [24]

---

[23] Mark Cuban on Why You Should Never Listen to Your Customers. Entrepreneur.com, December 20, 2011. Retrieved from http://www.entrepreneur.com/article/222501
[24] 20 Questions for Mark Cuban. Magbloom.com, February/March 2008. Retrieved from

Translation: Cuban doesn't believe any excuse exists for a passionate, hard-working entrepreneur to not succeed in business. Competition doesn't matter. The regulatory environment doesn't matter. Tax laws don't matter. The political climate doesn't matter. Your education doesn't matter. The state of the economy doesn't matter.

In fact, Cuban had to overcome a major crisis in the early days of MicroSolutions. An employee of the company embezzled $83,000 of the $85,000 the company had in the bank. Cuban started counting the months that MicroSolutions had been open, hoping it would last. He proudly boasts that after the theft, the company never had a month in which it lost money. [25]

Cuban not only believes that entrepreneurship is the key to his fulfillment, he also contends that it's the key to economic recovery in the U.S.

> "It's always the new idea that re-energizes this country. Industry,   manufacturing, transportation,   technology,   digital

---

http://www.magbloom.com/wp-content/uploads/2012/02/20Q_bloom10.pdf

[25] Mark Cuban, Billionaire. (Scared, Broke and Jobless). Subvertmagazine.com, September 10, 2012. Retrieved from http://www.subvertmagazine.com/blog/mark-cuban/

communications, etc., each changed how we lived and ignited our economy and standard of living. Tax policy has never done that. The American People have." [26]

"Entrepreneurs don't think about current economic times before they start a business. They think about the validity of their idea, the opportunity it affords them, and what it will take to be successful. If anything, many people will find themselves on the unfortunate side of job cuts and use it as motivation and a catalyst to start a business. I happen to believe that when your back is up against the wall, you will work harder and smarter to make your dreams come true." [27]

---

[26] The Cure to Our Economic Problems. Blog Maverick, October 23, 2008. Retrieved from http://blogmaverick.com/2012/09/17/the-cure-to-our-economic-problems-2/

[27] The Cure to Our Economic Problems. Blog Maverick, October 23, 2008. Retrieved from http://blogmaverick.com/2012/09/17/the-cure-to-our-economic-problems-2/

Chapter 3: The Visionary

In 1994, the World Wide Web was still a vast unknown. A select few had figured out how to market and advertise on the Internet, and fewer still had ascertained its potential as an entirely new business model and distribution channel.

By the middle of the year, there were less than 2,500 total websites in operation.

WhiteHouse.gov had just launched, as did a search engine known as Yahoo (the exclamation point hadn't appeared yet). America Online beckoned people to the new, exciting world of the Internet by sending sample CDs in the mail. At the time, there was no Google or eBay. Facebook was still over a decade away.

The late 90's mania surrounding Internet stocks was still on the horizon.

Most companies didn't have their own websites yet, nor did they provide widespread access to their office minions. The early adopters of the Internet logged on through their phone line, meaning that a website containing anything beyond basic text might take several minutes to load.

And yet, in 1994, college friends and soon-to-be lifelong business partners Todd Wagner and Mark Cuban predicted the Internet would evolve from offering just static text to providing real-time audio and video. This was 11 years before the debut of YouTube, which only allowed people to watch recorded video. Someday, they believed, people would look to their computers for live entertainment and sports programming instead of their televisions.

Their prediction came true, in part, because they followed one of Cuban's edicts for entrepreneurship. Quoting from technology luminary Alan Kay, Cuban believes: "The best way to predict the future is to invent it." [28]

According to accounts, Wagner pitched the idea of AudioNet to Cuban: Bringing live sporting events to the Internet so that people could listen to the games they wanted to. It would be a revolution, allowing fans to follow their teams anywhere in the world, so long as they had an Internet connection.

As savvy entrepreneurs, they did what many web companies failed to do… fill a real consumer need.

---

[28] Mark Cuban on Why You Should Never Listen to Your Customers. Entrepreneur.com, December 20, 2011. Retrieved from http://www.entrepreneur.com/article/222501

After all, did anybody really want to buy dog food over the Internet?

Specifically, the two men addressed one of their own needs. They wanted to follow the games of their alma mater, Indiana University. But one was hard-pressed at the time to find a Hoosier basketball game on in the Dallas market, unless ESPN or another network broadcast it nationally.

With such a mobile society, thousands of sports fans were now living far away from the teams they grew up with or supported in college. Prior to their company, Cuban and Wagner's only recourse was to call a friend who had access to an Indiana radio broadcast and have that person hold the phone up to the radio.

AudioNet was born in 1995, with a $5,000 investment, and the partners set up shop in a spare bedroom in Cuban's house. They purchased a Packard Bell PC, networking equipment and a high-speed Internet connection.

Soon they had persuaded a Dallas radio station to allow them to record broadcasts, which Cuban and Wagner would digitize and post on their website. A few months later they brought live broadcasts to the site by hooking up a radio tuner to the sound card in the computer.

Cuban explained during a 1999 interview with *VideoMaker Magazine* that the mission of his and Wagner's company was to turn the Internet into a broadcast medium. "We have put together the technology, infrastructure and software, and have aggregated content in order to aggregate audience. With this base, we offer content creators the ability to put their products of all kinds in front of an audience at a minimal cost." [29]

Interest quickly grew. Cuban and Wagner gave a 5 percent stake to Host Communications, which had the broadcast rights to 12 NCAA basketball teams and the NCAA men's basketball tournament, also known as March Madness. Then, they managed to sign exclusive agreements with most major colleges and universities and the National Football League, which allowed them to live stream the Super Bowl.

AudioNet soon expanded beyond sports and news broadcasts into business services, when they provided Internet broadcasting of conference calls, investor conferences, stockholder meetings and training sessions. At its peak, the company had deals with over 300 radio stations, 40 television stations, 400 sports teams, and 600 business customers.

---

[29] The Future of Video on the Internet. Blog Maverick, June 7, 2012. Retrieved from http://blogmaverick.com/2012/06/07/the-future-of-video-on-the-internet/

Despite its popularity, the company could not turn a profit. After spending a few million dollars of their own money, the partners sold shares in $30,000 increments to local investors and friends. Then they received another capital infusion through a private placement.

In 1998, the company was renamed Broadcast.com and went public with the goal of becoming the top broadcasting portal on the Internet. At the time of its IPO, Broadcast.com had fewer than $7 million in revenues, $28 million in equity, and an accumulated debt of nearly $10 million. The company had little to no chance of achieving profitability in the foreseeable future.

Of course, it was 1998. So a lack of profitability didn't stop enthusiastic investors from boosting the stock's value 249 percent on its first day of trading.

With more capital, Cuban and Wagner continued to expand the business. They purchased a company called Net Roadshow, which broadcast the roadshows that companies embarked upon when they were preparing for their initial public offerings.

Broadcast.com established a joint venture with a Japanese company to provide content in that language. Then it entered into a licensing agreement with Trimark Holdings to broadcast the company's entire film library. The company nearly crashed the Internet in February 1999 when Broadcast.com attracted 1.5 million viewers to watch a live Victoria's Secret fashion show.

The racy stunt helped put their website on the map.

How far ahead could Cuban think? In the aforementioned interview with VideoMaker in 1999, he essentially foretold the creation of YouTube, which would occur six years later. He said that it wouldn't be long until most of the streaming video on the Internet will be homemade videos.

"It will be so easy to present video to small audiences. Instead of the summer vacation or wedding video sitting on the shelf, we will post them on our family web sites so that grandma and grandpa can watch whenever they want. We will do the same with high schools posting their games, debates and school plays. It will be far more convenient than corralling everyone into the family room or making copies of the tape to send everywhere." [30]

---

[30] The Future of Video on the Internet. Blog Maverick, June 7, 2012. Retrieved from http://blogmaverick.com/2012/06/07/the-future-of-video-on-the-internet/

But the company itself may have been too far ahead of its time. Even with all its efforts, Broadcast.com couldn't get in the black. Its operating loss for 1998 was $15 million. So when Yahoo! approached Wagner and Cuban about acquiring the firm in April 1999, they spent little time debating the decision before agreeing to take the deal.

Competitors like Microsoft and America Online had moved in. Yahoo! was desperate to add Broadcast.com's capabilities to maintain its title as the leading web portal.

Yahoo! needed to upgrade from its regular text-only content to the multimedia capabilities that Broadcast.com offered. They purchased Cuban's and Wagner's brainchild for more than $5 billion.

Mark Cuban was officially a billionaire.

The duo joined the likes of Jeff Bezos, founder of Amazon.com, and others who invested in the potential of the Internet before most people recognized it. Yet, unlike many of those pioneers, Cuban and Wagner also recognized that the mania surrounding the Internet sector was not sustainable.

By February 2000, despite the fact that few of these companies had ever turned a simple profit, the market capitalization of Internet stocks accounted for 6 percent of the total market cap for all U.S. public companies. In two years, the entire sector had earned more 1000 percent returns. Part of the reason for the run-up was the rampant buying and selling of these stocks; about 20 percent of all publicly traded volume over this period was speculation in Internet stocks.[31] The demand for these issues continued to push share prices higher and higher.

Cuban and Wagner knew, like with anything in business, values can only go so high so fast before the bubble pops. Unable to turn a profit on Broadcast.com and with a sweet offer for the still unprofitable firm, the partners got out. And in keeping with their concern that Internet stocks were greatly overvalued, they hedged the Yahoo! stock used to make the acquisition and didn't lose the value of their shares when the acquiring company's stock tanked with the rest of the market. Had they not, the story of Mark Cuban would be a lot different today.

Cuban considers himself lucky. He also believes he created much of that luck on his own. He can see the future largely because he creates it -- at least in his corner of the universe. He doesn't jump on bandwagons; he launches them. He can study a new

---

[31] Dotcom Mania: The Rise and Fall of Internet Stock Prices. Eli Ofek and Matthew Richardson, National Bureau of Economic Research. December 2001. Retrieved from http://www.nber.org/papers/w8630.pdf?new_window=1

technology or emerging trend and visualize it five or 10 years down the road.

So if Mark Cuban were explaining the accomplishments of Broadcast.com, he wouldn't attribute the success to being ahead of the game. He would likely brag that the duo created a game that people, once they discovered it, wanted to play. And had this been the only time that Cuban invented a prosperous future, one could write it off as luck or good timing. But he did it again seven years later.

A blogger named James Altucher was contacted by Broadcast.com in 1997. At the time, Altucher ran a company called Reset, which was putting together the first regular live online production of a TV show, *The People's Court*. Broadcast.com wanted to use Reset's technology to do live streaming. Altucher later wrote about the interaction in a blog post titled "How I Helped Mark Cuban Make a Billion Dollars and the 5 Things I Learned from Him."

What he learned speaks to Cuban's visionary prowess:

> "Most people I speak to about Cuban say he was lucky. He created a company with minimal revenues in the internet video/audio space, had the biggest IPO in history at the time (1998), immediately put the company up for sale, sold to the biggest Internet

company (Yahoo!), and then sold all his shares at the very top. How did he know to sell at the top? Is that the 'luck' part everyone refers to? Or the fact that he started a company with no revs and was just 'lucky' it was at the right time (the Internet bubble?)

It wasn't luck at all. In chess there's a saying, 'only the good players are lucky.' Whenever a good player wins a game, the angry opponent often says, 'ahh, you were just lucky.' But it always seems the good player gets lucky more than the bad player.

He knew, probably five years in advance, that a bubble was occurring and this was the exact plan to maximize value from it. He probably extracted more from the initial Internet bubble than anyone else. It doesn't happen by luck that you sell at the top. You have to know five years in advance when that top will occur. And then have to have a very precise plan for being at the right spot at the right time at the very top." [32]

Cuban splurged on himself after collecting his payday from the sale of Broadcast.com. One of his acquisitions was a high-definition TV with a 100-inch projection screen. It cost him around $10,000. Just like with the Internet in 1994, HDTV in 2000 was still a novelty. In fact, Cuban recalls that only one channel on his new DirectTV package offered high-definition programming. It consisted of a continuous loop of about 90 minutes worth of animal footage and old sports reels.

Nobody was producing content because few believed that people would pony up for expensive TV sets just because they delivered high-quality pictures. It began as the classic chicken-and-egg scenario: Content providers needed consumers to adopt HDTV before they would invest in content, but consumers weren't going to buy sets without any content available.

That's when Cuban decided to launch the future of HDTV, instead of waiting for it to materialize. He had seen personal computers become affordable in his lifetime, so why wouldn't HDTV sets?

"And if the traditional media couldn't see that — well, it just opened the door for me," Cuban said of the coming HDTV revolution. [33]

---

[33] Heilemann, J. (2004). Mark Cuban's End Game. Business 2.0, 5(11), 46.

He teamed with veteran TV producer Philip Garvin and developed a new network: HDNet on satellite provider DirectTV, which launched in September 2001, just five days before the 9/11 terrorist attacks.

All of the network's original programming was produced in high definition. And though it didn't offer the breadth of programming one could find on the non-high-definition stations, it also bore no resemblance to that running loop he discovered on his satellite package. Months after HDNet launched, it aired exclusive hi-definition coverage of the U.S. invasion of Afghanistan. The following February, the network brought viewers high-definition video of the 2002 Winter Olympics in Salt Lake City.

Its regular programming included space shuttle launches, travel shows, news programs, and male-oriented shows featuring young women in bikinis.

Over the years to come, HDNet would broadcast National Hockey League games, Major League Soccer, auto racing, mixed-martial arts fights, lower-level professional wrestling and the upstart United Football League, which Cuban initially thought about investing in before backing out. Syndicated reruns of cult TV shows filled out the schedule.

Within three years, Cuban had invested more than $100 million into the network. That bought 1,200 hours of original programming filmed in high definition and a robust library of licensed content. The network employed eight crews shooting HD video around the globe, helping to fill the 24/7 network with 15 hours of new, original programming each week.

As his network was growing, so was the industry. Prices for sets were dropping, just as Cuban predicted. In 2002, consumers bought 2.5 million HDTV sets, and another 4 million in 2003. [34]

Cuban later added a second HD network: HDNet Movies, which brought high-definition, commercial-free films to subscribers. The network showed older films that it has transferred in 1080i high definition or shot originally in the format. Many films shown on HDNet Movies had never before been released in HD on other networks.

Of course, high-definition TV is no longer a novelty. HD sets are now about all one can buy, and HD programming has become the rule, not the exception. This evolution has forced Cuban to rebrand his network and position it in a much different way.

---

[34] Gallagher, L. (2004). The Big Picture. (cover story). Forbes, 173(4), 78-82.

Recently renamed AXS TV, the network is now cast as a provider of live television, covering sports (primarily Mixed Martial Arts), pop culture, music, fashion, and other areas. One of its feature programs is still *Dan Rather Reports*, an investigative news magazine nominated for an Emmy award for Outstanding Investigative Journalism.

HDNet was the foundation for a much larger vision Cuban and Wagner would develop during the first decade of the new millennium. The partners have since created a vertically integrated media and entertainment empire with individual properties that represent each aspect of the entertainment supply chain.

Their new company, **2929 Entertainment**, can develop, produce and distribute TV and film programming. The firm owns film distributor Magnolia Pictures, Landmark Theaters and the AXS TV cable networks, among other properties.

With the pieces in place, Cuban and Wagner have sought to create history again, this time by changing all the rules of established media: how it's distributed, how it's marketed and how it's promoted. And in their quest, they are encountering critics who think their ideas will fail, protectionists who want them to fail because it could ruin old business models, and those who anxiously await the new world Cuban envisions.

If there's a lesson would-be entrepreneurs could learn from Cuban's visionary ways, it's this: Success is never about the idea itself. It's about the hard work you perform to take the idea from vision to reality.

"Over the last 20 years, I've always been about what's new, what's next and how am I getting there first. It's a sprint and I have to keep on running 150 miles per hour. It's an adventure." [35]

"Everyone has ideas," Cuban has said. "The hard part is doing the homework to know if the idea could work in an industry, then doing the preparation to be able to execute on the idea. Otherwise, someone who knows more and works harder will kick your ass."

For Mark Cuban, execution is everything.

---

[35] Mark Cuban profile. Business Innovation Factory. Retrieved from
http://businessinnovationfactory.com/iss/innovators/mark-cuban

Chapter 4: The Entertainer

Few industries have evolved as rapidly, and have as much uncertainty, as the media business.

It's this rampant fluidity that makes media the perfect haven for an opportunistic, visionary entrepreneur who is driven to succeed but can afford to fail. A person like Mark Cuban.

Consider the developments in mass media over the last 30 years. For the better part of the 20th century, consumers essentially had four options for media consumption.

The print world, including books, magazines, and newspapers, owned a mass media monopoly for generations. Then, recorded music and radio industries took share in the first decades of the century, but not until the 1920s did technological advancements make them more commercially viable. Broadcast television took off in the late 1940s and early 1950s. For the next 30 years, these mediums were about the only options for people to receive information and enjoy content in their homes.

In the late 1970s and early 1980s, the media world began its fragmentation and things would never be the same for consumers. Pay-TV, including basic cable, satellite TV, and subscription channels like HBO, gave viewers more options. Networks like ESPN, CNN, and MTV provided specific niche programming for targeted audiences, a trend that would only get more pronounced as bandwidth opened up and more networks were born.

The Internet opened up an entirely new world beginning in the early 1990s. Much of the content people used to have to pay for suddenly became free. It delivered music and video digitally. It signaled the slow death of physical media, like cassettes, CDs, DVDs and videotapes.

Despite all of these recent advancements, Mark Cuban has the foresight to know that today's devices will soon be obsolete.

> "How many times have we heard someone talk about the future of media and they immediately use their child as an example of what we all will experience in the future?
> Think about your own childhood. Do you still use ANY of the same devices? Still have that cassette player? Still burning those CDs? That Walkman that wowed your parents still wowing anyone? You still carrying your boom box on your shoulder like Radio Raheem? Of course not.

If you think that the tech your young kids are using today is any reflection on what will be used in the future, even in the near future, you are mistaken. It's also short changing the intellect of every kid 18 and under. You don't think they can come up with something better? The reality is that we do not live in the world we were born into. Things change."[36]

Which may explain why Mark Cuban, following the sale of Broadcast.com, has focused more of his energy on content than on distribution. While immersing himself in technology made him a millionaire, selling things that people want to listen to and watch made him a billionaire.

For Mark Cuban, it was back to Hollywood; not in the physical sense, but through a variety of investments in the movie and TV business.

This also meant a reunion with business partner Todd Wagner. The two joined forces to create a vertically integrated entertainment company. But again, Cuban wasn't going to operate his media company like everybody else did.

---

[36] The Dumbest Words in New Media. Blog Maverick, May 10, 2013. Retrieved from http://blogmaverick.com/2013/05/10/the-dumbest-words-in-new-media/

In addition to HDNet, which was renamed **AXS TV** in 2012, and **HDNet Movies**, the partners' company owns: **2929 Productions**, a film production house, **Magnolia Pictures**, a film distributor, and **Landmark Theatres**, a 227-screen theater chain. Each of these companies fits under the umbrella of 2929 Entertainment, and each company represents a unique piece of the movie and TV value and supply chain.

"We realized that because we are vertically integrated, with AXS TV, Landmark Theaters, Magnolia Pictures and 2929 Films, not only could we make, distribute, show and sell movies, but we didn't have to play by all the old Hollywood rules," Cuban said. "I decided to look at the technology opportunities that would allow us to change how the game was played that others may not be aware of." [37]

In the beginning, Cuban struggled to get major cable providers to pony up for HDNet. Some say his antics as an NBA owner had cost him distribution. Several NBA team owners also control cable systems, and the theory went that they refused to carry HDNet because of his intrusion on their fraternity. Others claim it was simply a combination of a lack of

---

[37] Exclusive Conversation with Mark Cuban. The Legacy Series, October 16, 2012.
http://jobslegacy.wordpress.com/tag/innovation/

compelling content and the price Cuban was asking to carry his network. [38]

The same companies that, early on, had refused to carry HDNet turned around and joined forces to create their own high-definition network, called MOJO HD. Many in the industry referred to the network as the "the Cuban killer." [39] But it was MOJO that met its own demise, lasting only 18 months before it was shuttered on December 1, 2008.

Cuban lured the large providers eventually, but they didn't subscribe for long.

As the economy tanked, cable subscribers fled for satellite providers and the cost of premium channels like ESPN skyrocketed, some cable companies cut the cord on HDNet. In May 2009, the network lost access to Time Warner Cable. Later than year, RCN, Mediacom and MetroCast Cablevision stopped carrying the network. In February 2011, HDNet was dropped by Cox.

---

[38] Leonard, D. (2007). MARK CUBAN MAY BE A BILLIONAIRE, BUT WHAT HE REALLY NEEDS IS RESPECT. Fortune, 156(8), 172-182.

[39] Leonard, D. (2007). MARK CUBAN MAY BE A BILLIONAIRE, BUT WHAT HE REALLY NEEDS IS RESPECT. Fortune, 156(8), 172-182.

Several major television providers in Canada also opted not to carry Cuban's network during the same period.

The birth of AXS TV

Now with high-definition TV no longer a novelty, Cuban needed a different hook to attract viewers to his network. With services like Netflix and Hulu, as well as the Internet sites of the major TV and cable networks, recorded programming was quickly migrating from television to the web.

Cuban, ever the visionary, correctly figured this trend would likely continue given the proliferation of tablets and smartphones that allow users to watch recorded programs anywhere they can get an Internet connection. He realized that live programming is the last type of content that is still best delivered on television.

For sports, breaking news and live special events like awards shows and concerts, people will still gravitate to their televisions. What's more, the emergence of social media, especially Twitter, gives viewers an outlet to share their thoughts and opinions with their friends and followers as things unfold.

Live events, Cuban has ascertained, are the only programming left that can draw large simultaneous audiences while helping create buzz via social media.

So in July 2012, Cuban's entertainment company teamed with AEG, Ryan Seacrest Media and Creative Artists Agency to launch AXS TV. The new network replaced HDNet on satellite and cable packages.

AXS TV is branded as the "premier destination for live events, breaking news, and as-they-are-happening trends in the worlds of pop culture, music, fashion, and entertainment."

From multi-day festivals to stadium tours to club acts, AXS TV delivers an unparalleled shared experience for fans of all genres. With multiple live concerts weekly, AXS TV is the number one destination for artists and their fans to experience and share a pure live event in the world of music and pop culture.

"From show creation and development to rehearsals, sound-check and performance and right thru the after-party, AXS TV viewers get an immersive look into their favorite acts touring today from across the globe," read the press release.

The network uses AEG's L.A. LIVE production facilities and has access to the mega-promoter's other worldwide venues.

One example of the network's live music programming is *The World's Greatest Tribute Bands*, a weekly series broadcast live from the Roxy Theatre on Sunset Boulevard in West Hollywood. The show features a different band each week paying tribute to classic artists such as David Bowie, Bon Jovi, Led Zeppelin, Iron Maiden and Pink Floyd.

Live comedy shows from New York's Gotham Comedy Club were also added to the mix.
AXS TV provides some live news content. In April 2013, the network inked a deal with AOL to simulcast several hours of its live web news stream, HuffPost Live. [40]

The movie business

Magnolia Pictures has distributed numerous independent films, including James Marsh's critically acclaimed 2008 documentary *Man on Wire*, about tightrope walker Philippe Petit. The company's home entertainment arm sometimes releases films simultaneously with their theatrical debut via HDNet Movies.

---

[40] AOL's HuffPost Live Gets Shot on Cable with Mark Cuban's AXS TV. Ad Age digital, April 28, 2013. Retrieved from http://adage.com/article/digital/aol-s-huffpost-live-shot-tv-mark-cuban-s-axs-tv/241164/

In 2003, Cuban and Wagner purchased Landmark Theatres from bankruptcy protection. Founded in 1974, Landmark is the largest chain dedicated to showing independent films and its fare skews toward foreign flicks and intellectual avant-garde films. In addition to the initial purchase, Cuban and Wagner spent millions upgrading the chain's facilities.

Today, Landmark operates 227 screens in 50 theaters located in 21 U.S. markets. Many of its theaters are historic landmarks, including the Trivoli in St. Louis, the Inwood in Dallas and the Oriental in Milwaukee.

Cuban's belief in the customer experience shows at a typical Landmark. Movies are digitally projected. The concession stand features gourmet cuisine. Customers can buy DVDs, books and CDs at the theater and several of its facilities feature couches and loveseats. In 2010, the chain introduced environmentally friendly EcoSelect popcorn bags at all of its locations.

With all the pieces of the film creation and distribution channel in place, the company wanted to test a new method of distributing movies. The traditional business model is to release a new film in theaters, followed by a DVD release a few months later, then the movie becomes available on pay-TV movie channels. Cuban and Wagner wanted to test a simultaneous release, giving consumers a choice of how they wanted to see a movie and offering that choice at the same time: in a theater, on DVD, and on HDNet.

They signed up Academy Award-winning director Steven Soderbergh to direct *Bubble*, a murder mystery involving workers in a doll factory located in a struggling small town. Released in February 2006 on a $1.6 million budget, the movie struggled at the box office due to boycotts by theater chains threatened by Cuban's new distribution model. The movie reportedly grossed just $145,000 in its theater run.

Then in 2011, Cuban and Wagner put Landmark and Magnolia up for sale, however they never completed a transaction involving the properties.

"Prices for entertainment properties are up," Cuban said regarding the proposed sale. "If we don't get the price and premium we want, we are happy to continue to make money from the properties."

The company's production house, 2929 Productions, has enjoyed both critical and financial success.

Its biggest achievement was the 2005 release of *Good Night, and Good Luck*, which told the story of the public battle pitting CBS newsmen Edward R. Murrow and Fred Friendly against Wisconsin Senator Joseph McCarthy during the Communism panic of the 1950s. The film featured Jeff Daniels, George Clooney and Robert Downey Jr.

Clooney also directed the film, and *Good Night* earned six Academy Award nominations, including Best Picture, Best Director and Best Original Screenplay. It was also named the Movie of the Year for 2006 by the American Film Institute. Produced for only $7.5 million, the released grossed over $31 million in the U.S. box office.

A year later, the company released another critically acclaimed hit, *Akeelah and the Bee*, about a girl from South Los Angeles trying to qualify for the National Spelling Bee. Its domestic box office gross was nearly $19 million. That same year, 2929 released *The Smartest Guys in the Room*, about the Enron scandal, which earned an Academy Award nomination for Best Documentary.

Cuban and the rest of the production company seem little interested in big budget CGI blockbusters. Among 2929's production credits are *Rejoice and Shout*, a 2010 documentary about the history of Gospel music; *Casino Jack and the United States of Money*, a 2010 investigation into D.C. lobbyist Jack Abramoff; and *Gonzo*, a 2008 documentary detailing the life of famed journalist Hunter S. Thompson.

Look closely at these and other production credits, and a familiar Mark Cuban theme emerges. Celebrate the underdogs and those who champion their cause. Expose the atrocities committed by corrupt institutions. Cuban says the content he provides, be it TV or movies, is just about good business.

> "I'm just looking for programming that I think is going to be memorable, that is going to impact people personally, and stuff that people will think is funny -- kind of like a baby HBO from a content perspective. Most companies, most media companies or public companies, are geared toward earnings per share, and that drives everything: hitting the numbers, hitting the quarter mark...Everybody else does nothing more creative than following the trend. It's like: Let's do another poker show. Now let's extend that to blackjack. Now let's mix blackjack with poker. Now let's pimp my ride, let's pimp my house, let's get tattoos, let's get bounty hunters. If everybody else is doing it, I don't want to do it. Rather than trying to grovel for an extra share of viewers like most media companies do these days, I'd rather just

throw it up against the wall and take some chances." [41]

And yet, Cuban has written in the past about how the economics of movie making and marketing consume him. So much so that he issued an open challenge to readers of his blog: Develop a way to convince five million people to see a film in a theater without spending so much on marketing that it barely breaks even during its theatrical release. Cuban wrote that he'd offer a job to the person who could solve the dilemma.

> "It's not unusual to spend 8, 10, 12 dollars PER PERSON that goes to a movie in the opening weekend. Shoot, it's not unusual for studios to spend that much per person to get people to go to the theater through a movie's entire run!
>
> How crazy is it to spend more on marketing than the revenue received when they go to the movie? It's double crazy because that revenue is split with the theater. So if a studio spends 12 bucks to get someone to go to the theater,

---

[41] What I've Learned: Mark Cuban. Esquire.com, November 17, 2008. Retrieved from http://www.esquire.com/features/what-ive-learned/ESQ1206BBCUBAN_182_1

they might only be getting 4 dollars back in return.

You would think that there has to be a better way than spending 1x, 2x, 3x or more times the initial revenue received opening weekend or week? Right?

So if you want a job, and have a great idea on how to market movies in a completely different way, if your idea works for any and all kinds of movies, if it changes the dynamics and the economics of promoting movies, email it or post it. If it's new and unique, I want to hear about it. If it's a different way of doing the same thing you have seen before, it probably won't get you a job, but feel free to try.

So go for it. Come up with a great idea that I want to use and I will come up with a job for you to make that idea happen.[42]

Cuban provided his own potential solution two years later, when he blogged about an idea for giving away movie soundtrack downloads or other digital content

---

[42] The Movie Business Challenge. Blog Maverick, July 23, 2006. Retrieved from http://blogmaverick.com/2006/07/23/the-movie-business-challenge/

with the purchase of a theater ticket. Developing ways to give people more value for their entertainment dollar has always come easily to Mark Cuban, from the early wet t-shirt contests at his college bar to his most publicized venture, as owner (and chief mascot) of the NBA's Dallas Mavericks.

Chapter 5: The Rooter

On an early winter afternoon in 1999, Cuban entertained an assembly of Harvard Business School alumni at the Dallas Petroleum Club. The club was founded in 1934 as a fraternity of oil men. It bills itself as "one of the finest private clubs in the country in which its members, who include oil and gas executives in the industry, business, finance, education, government, medicine, and the arts, cherish the club because of the personal attention and exceptional service they receive once they enter its quarters."

Business casual dress is required at all times, except in the bar, and cell phone usage is prohibited in the main dining and bar area. [43] It doesn't sound like the kind of place Mark Cuban could spend a lot of time in, given his wheeling-dealing ways and penchant for wearing faded blue jeans and T-shirts.

Though it was set up as a speech, the session became more of a storytelling session, with the bankers and lawyers peppering Cuban with questions about things

---

[43]

http://www.thedallaspetroleumclub.com/viewCustomPage.aspx?id=3

they had heard or read about the newest member of the billionaire's club.

One of the attendees brought up Cuban's purchase of a $40 million Gulfstream airplane, a transaction Cuban claims to have conducted via email. Fresh off the sale of Broadcast.com, Cuban had just recently found himself with $2.5 billion in wealth and an appetite to spend it.

"It was one of the three things I wanted. The first was the house," Cuban told the gathering, referring to the 10-bedroom, 24,000-square-foot Dallas mansion he purchased from a subprime mortgage lender that was in financial trouble. He got the house for $15 million. [44]

"The second was the plane."

An eager voice from the crowed piped up: "What's the third?"

"Ah, ah, ah!" Cuban replied. "I'm keeping that private just now." [45]

---

[44] (2005). MAVERICK MOGUL. Fast Company, (101), 70.

[45] The Billionaire. Esquire.com, April 1, 2000. Retrieved from http://www.esquire.com/features/billionaire-cuban-sound-0400

On January 14, 2000, Mark Cuban became the majority owner of the Dallas Mavericks of the National Basketball Association, buying the team for $280 million. Cuban wasn't the first fan to buy a team just because he could. But whereas many newbie sports owners struggle to adjust to the different business model of professional athletics, Cuban had the opposite experience.

Prior to Mark Cuban's ownership, the Mavericks were one of the worst franchises in the NBA. Launched in 1980 after millionaire Donald Carter secured the franchise, the Mavericks ended a seven-year absence of professional basketball in Dallas.

From 1967 to 1973, the Dallas Chaparrals played in the American Basketball Association, eventually moving to San Antonio to join the NBA and become the Spurs. The Mavericks began play in the brand new Reunion Arena and quickly became a marginally successful franchise by qualifying for the playoffs six times during the 1980s.

But the 1990s were a different story. They suffered nine consecutive losing seasons prior to Cuban's purchase. From the 1990-91 season through the 1998-99 campaign, the Mavericks won just 28 percent of their games, the worst record of any team in any professional sport during that period. In two seasons combined, from 1992 to 1994, the team won 24 games in TOTAL, while losing 140.

Cuban seemed to make an immediate impact. The team started the 1999-2000 season much the same as recent years, with a record of 9-23 when Cuban took over. The Mavericks quickly rebounded and finished the season 31-19, including 9-1 in the month of April to finish the overall season at 40-42, their best record in 10 years. Although the team missed the playoffs, the foundation was set for a bright future.

Right out of the gate, Cuban sought to improve the climate of the organization. He upgraded the players' hotel and travel accommodations on the road, replaced the bench chairs with more plush models and equipped each team member's locker-room cubicle with a personal stereo, flat-screen monitor, DVD player and Sony PlayStation. He hired eight assistant coaches, about double the normal staff size in the NBA. He paid attention to the morale of the team's office workers, providing them free soft drinks, ice cream bars and massages. Even the little details he addressed, such as replacing the cheap NBA standard towels in the locker room with ones that cost $20 each. [46]

---

[46] Hoffer, R. (2011). NEW DIRECTIONS. Sports Illustrated, 66.

The quick turnaround and his fresh perspective endeared Cuban to long-suffering Mavericks fans. In their eyes, he was spending the kind of money necessary to field a better team on the court. He continued to cheer from the same seats he had in years past, showcasing his energy and enthusiasm for the team. He would regularly shell out $2,000 for after-game drinks at the arena bar when the team won. He reportedly handed out free tickets to attractive women to improve the atmosphere as well.

Cuban engaged with fans personally by encouraging them to email him. He has responded to thousands of those messages, and would often ask fans whether they received good service from the arena ushers and concession workers.

The next season the club finished 53-29 en route to its first playoff appearance in 11 years. Next year the Mavericks moved into the American Airlines Center and promptly set a franchise best record at 57-25, including an NBA best road record of 27-14. That record didn't stand long, as the Mavericks won 60 games the next year, 58 in 2004-2005 and 60 again the year after that.

In 2006, Dallas made its first ever trip to the NBA Finals, winning the first two games of the series before losing the next four and surrendering the championship to the Miami Heat. Game 5 was especially tough, as a ballistic Cuban reportedly shouted in Stern's direction that the league was fixed. Though he denied saying that, he was still fined $250,000. Like a true fan, Cuban was devastated by the series loss; he didn't come out of his house for three weeks and he contemplated selling the team. [47]

But the team's success would continue. Dallas set an all-time team best regular season record the following year at 67-15, but stumbled in the first round of the playoffs, losing to the 8th-seeded Golden State Warriors. The Warriors were coached by Don Nelson, who was the Mavericks' coach when Cuban bought the team. Their relationship started out well, but deteriorated beginning in the 2003 playoffs when Cuban questioned Nelson's reluctance to play an injured Dirk Nowitzki, the squad's top player. It continued during Nelson's contract negotiations. Nelson agreed to coach the team for three seasons, then work for the team as a consultant. That agreement was never fulfilled, and Nelson took the job with Golden State. He later successfully sued Cuban for $6 million in back pay. Cuban the fan took center stage following the playoff loss to the Warriors, accusing his former coach of using

---

[47] Leonard, D. (2007). MARK CUBAN MAY BE A BILLIONAIRE, BUT WHAT HE REALLY NEEDS IS RESPECT. Fortune, 156(8), 172-182.

information he gleaned from his time with the Mavericks to pull off the upset. [48]

The Mavericks looked to have a strong team heading into the 2010-2011 season, its 31st as a franchise. But while making the playoffs seemed like a foregone conclusion, the depth of the league's top contenders would make it an uphill climb to earn that elusive first championship. The Kobe Bryant-led Los Angeles Lakers were the two-time defending champs. The San Antonio Spurs had arguably the most consistently proficient organization in the league, and the upstart Oklahoma City Thunder boasted the best young player in the game, Kevin Durant. In the Eastern Conference, LeBron James, considered the best player in the league, joined the Miami Heat along with Chris Bosh to team up with perennial all-start Dwyane Wade. Many considered "The Big Three" the odds-on favorite to win the title.

Led by Nowitzki, Shawn Marion, Tyson Chandler and Jason Kidd, the Mavericks finished the regular season 57-25, third place in the Western Conference behind San Antonio and the Lakers. Dallas took a six-game series from the Portland Trail Blazers in the first

---

[48] Ex-Mavs Coach Nelson Wins $6.3M in Arbitration Against Cuban. ESPN.com, August 1, 2008. Retrieved from http://sports.espn.go.com/nba/news/story?id=351 4135

round, then stunned the Lakers with a four-game sweep in the conference semifinals.

In the conference finals against Oklahoma City, Dallas won three straight by coming from behind in the fourth quarter each time to win the series 4-1. That set up an NBA Finals matchup with the Miami Heat. For Cuban, Nowitski and guard Jason Terry, the only two players remaining from the 2006 runner-up squad, it was a chance to avenge the bitter Finals defeat from five years prior. For the entire Dallas organization, it was an opportunity to shock a world that had already crowned the "Big Three" before the season began and to win its first championship.

After dropping the first game in Miami, the Mavericks were on the brink of falling behind two games to none when the Heat held a 15-point lead with 7 minutes left. But the Mavericks rallied and took the lead for good on a game-winning layup by Nowitzki with 4 seconds remaining.

Following that dramatic finish, Dallas won two of three games held in its home arena and clinched the series in Game 6, held in Miami.

In what was probably one of the greatest moments of his life, Cuban decided to step back. While it's customary for the commissioner to hand the trophy to the team's owner or top executive, Cuban instead allowed Donald Carter, who started the franchise, to accept the trophy on the team's behalf.

Mavs Fan For Life

Few people buy sports franchises as an investment. They are bought by fans who want to be part of the action. Cuban is different in that regard. While winning is the top priority, he has also turned the Mavericks into a viable business.

As the typical fan who identifies himself with his favorite teams, Cuban has always been a winner. There was perhaps no better place to grow up as a sports fan in the 1970s than Pittsburgh. The Steelers won four Super Bowls during Cuban's teenage years. The Pirates won the World Series in 1971 and 1979, with two other division titles during the decade. The NHL's Penguins fielded strong teams that consistently qualified for the playoffs.

The winning continued in college when his alma mater Indiana Hoosiers won the 1981 NCAA national men's basketball championship the year Cuban graduated. Things started out well his first years in Dallas, as both the Cowboys and Mavericks were perennial playoff contenders. But then the winning stopped for a time. The Cowboys suffered through several losing seasons, going 1-15 in 1989 before winning three Super Bowls in the 1990s.

That left the Mavericks, the team Cuban was most passionate about, having invested every year in season tickets. He signs his blogs MFFL, which stands for Mavs Fan For Life. The abbreviation is also on his vehicle license plates.

Having endured a decade of losing, Cuban wanted to field a winner immediately; there was no time for long-term rebuilding efforts.

Despite his role as a team owner, Cuban never shed his identity as a fan. Fans relate to him because in his soul, he's one of them. Obviously his billions of dollars in net worth puts him in a different social class. But Cuban doesn't behave like the "wealthy" fan. He doesn't sit courtside just to be seen. He doesn't treat the game like a social gathering with his country club friends or as the setting for closing his next business deal. Instead, he's truly engaged in the action happening on the court. He doesn't take up prime seats from a true fan, because he is a true fan. He appears to follow the Mavericks as a team more than he follows the team as a business. Just like any true fan, he shares, without any kind of filter, his opinion on what the Lakers should do with Kobe Bryant, or why he thinks the Miami Heat are the "evil empire."

Cuban berates the officials anytime a call goes against his team. If he wasn't one of the richest men in the world, one could easily picture the scruffy billionaire hanging out with his buddies at a Buffalo Wild Wings watching multiple sporting events at once, debating the greatest shooters in basketball and hitting on the waitress.

As the owner, Cuban has the authority to do what many fans wish they could: Storm into the locker room after a lackluster performance and lay in to the offending players, or inserting himself into the team huddle during games. And he can share his criticism of officiating with millions by talking to a reporter, tweeting to his 1.7 million followers or sharing his disgust on his blog.

At the same time, he represents a league that does not take kindly to his antics. While the average fan can yell whatever he wants to the officials, Cuban's criticism has cost him millions over the years. He once criticized the head of league officials by stating he how wouldn't trust the official to "manage a Dairy Queen." That drew the ire of both the league and Dairy Queen. But media savvy as he is, Cuban took the opportunity to work a day in a Dallas-area DQ, serving up cones and shakes to many appreciative Maverick fans.

With all of his success in his other ventures, Cuban's only failure, perhaps, is his inability to add to his sports empire. Cuban has attempted on several more occasions to mix business with sports. In 2006, he teamed with fellow Pittsburgh native and former NFL quarterback Dan Marino to bid $170 million for the Pittsburgh Penguins hockey franchise, but he was rejected.

Three years later, Cuban was prepared to spend a princely sum on one of the marquee franchises in all of professional sports: the Chicago Cubs.

"It's a team that represents so much to so many, with such a unique legacy, that when the opportunity arose, I decided to go for it," Cuban wrote in his blog on January 6, 2009.

Cuban really wanted to own the Cubs and thought his chances were good. He offered what he believed was a competitive price. One published report indicated that Cuban submitted the highest bid at $1.3 billion. Some claimed that Cuban never had a chance, regardless of his bid. The reason: Major League Baseball, like all the major sports leagues, have to approve any new team owners by a vote of the league's other owners.

Sources told ESPN that MLB owners feared Cuban would drive up player salaries by overspending for talent and exacerbate the gap between wealthy teams like the New York Yankees and Boston Red Sox and the league's also-rans. [49]

Cuban said that wasn't the case. He did desire to invest his resources to make the Cubs perennial contenders like he did the Mavericks, but at the same time did not want to spend as much on talent as the Red Sox and Yankees. He stated in his blog that he didn't want to pass on the expense of a bloated payroll to the team's loyalists. In fact, he believed he didn't have to spend that much, because he only had to compete with those clubs in a World Series. The rivals within the Cubs' division, the National League Central, were by and large not big spenders.

"My plans were to spend to win, not to spend for spending's sake," Cuban wrote in his blog. "[In my humble opinion], the money I could save being in the 2nd tier of payroll could be invested in scouting and development. I made this clear to any and all of the owners that I spoke to across the league. Of course that didn't stop some from trying to convince some owners otherwise."

---

[49] Report: 'Zero Chance' that MLB will Accept Cuban's Cubs Bid. ESPN.com, November 8, 2008. Retrieved from http://sports.espn.go.com/mlb/news/story?id=3687712

In the end, according to Cuban, his quest to buy the popular franchise ended because of the economic collapse of 2008. While Cuban may be a rabid fan, he's also an astute businessman. The adage of "buy low, sell high," applies to sports franchises.

He bought the Mavericks when they worth very little during a time when money was abundant. Trying to buy the Cubs in 2008 was the exact opposite; a franchise worth as much as it ever had been during a time when economic uncertainty carried the day. Before the financial crisis, Cuban was looking to finance the deal with short-term loans, then refinance at the end of each term, a common practice before the crisis. Once the crisis hit, there was no guarantee Cuban could refinance in a few years. His other option was to bring on more investors and pay cash for the Cubs. But he wrote in his blog that he was not about to spend that much in cash.

"Once the credit crisis hit, the value of cash went through the roof. It was not just a matter of how much the Cubs were worth, it was also a matter of how much more money I could earn with that cash. Cash was and is king," Cuban explained. "Distressed investment opportunities were rolling in the door that could make me multiples of what any sports team could. I could not see any scenario where the Cubs were worth anywhere near the numbers that had been discussed in the media." [50]

A year after that bid, Cuban and his investment group were outbid in an attempt to buy the Texas Ranger baseball team, which at the time was being auctioned by a bankruptcy court. Cuban was outbid by a group headed by former Rangers pitcher and Hall-of-Famer Nolan Ryan.

In 2011, the New York Mets, mired in the Bernie Madoff Ponzi scheme, were put up for sale. Cuban said he would consider jumping into the bidding only if the current owners called him; he wasn't going to chase it like he did his other baseball pursuits. In 2012, Cuban made another failed attempt to get into baseball by bidding for the Los Angeles Dodgers. Cuban was eliminated early in the process with a bid that was too low.

"The economics got so out of control because the Dodgers' TV deal's up for bid and so there's a lot of groups coming in going, 'This TV deal's worth so much money that we're gonna pay whatever it takes to get the Dodgers.' And so they're buying the TV

---

[50] The Cubs. Blog Maverick, January 6, 2009. Retrieved from http://blogmaverick.com/2009/01/06/the-cubs/

rights deal first and the team second," Cuban said at the time. [51]

Cuban also flirted with professional football, but not the big-time National Football League.

The United Football League was a four-team league that kicked off in 2009 in second-tier markets not served by the more established NFL. Cuban originally expressed interest in joining the UFL ownership group, but ultimately decided to limit his participation to broadcasting games on his HDNet network.

Cuban loaned the league money in 2011. This was at a time when the NFL and its players association were at a standstill in labor negotiations, which threatened to cancel some or all of the season. In the end, the NFL made peace with the players, and the UFL folded shortly later. Cuban filed a $5 million lawsuit to recoup the loan he made to the UFL.

Cuban loves sports. He also loves business and making money. Sometimes those two things are at odds. As much of a salesman as he is, and as much as he could charge for Mavericks tickets, the fan in him

---

[51] Cuban Explains Losing Out on Dodgers. CBSSports.com, January 30, 2012. Retrieved from http://www.cbssports.com/mcc/blogs/entry/22297882/34631046

wants everybody to have a chance to enjoy a live game every now and then. That explains why the Mavericks set aside 1,500 seats for 10 home games that sell for just $2, about the cost of a 20-ounce soda at a convenience store. Fans who attend games solo can buy their seat for as little as $5. [52]

Cuban eloquently wrote about the dichotomy between fan and businessman in one of his Maverick Blog posts:

> "When you own a professional sports team it doesn't take long to realize that owning a team is unlike owning any other business. On one hand the competitive side of ownership is a driving force. I want to win championships. I want to win every game. Not just for me, but for the entire organization and all of North Texas and for Mavs fans everywhere. Thirteen years into owning the Mavs and it still hurts every time we lose. I still have a hard time sleeping after any game we lose.
>
> But to some Mavs fans the Mavs are more than just a game. They are a release. They are a connection to other family members. They

[52] 20 Questions for Mark Cuban. Magbloom.com, February/March 2008. Retrieved from http://www.magbloom.com/wp-content/uploads/2012/02/20Q_bloom10.pdf

are an escape from the realities of a very difficult life. There are fans who love the Mavs because it makes their lives better. There are not many businesses that can begin to have that kind of impact on their customers/fans.

It is this connection that also drives me to make sure that every Mavs game is about far more than basketball. I want to make sure that every time any fan walks into the American Airlines Center they know that they will feel special. They will have a special experience. They will have an emotional connection… It is a special trust that is incumbent on me and all Mavs employees to live up to. It is expensive to deliver on this goal. But it is worth every penny. No matter what it costs. I'm proud of the fact that the Mavs spend, by all accounts, more than any other team in any sport around the world on in game entertainment and experience. While other teams worry about wi-fi and apps, we worry about creating an experience that is unique to Mavs games." [53]

---

[53] The Mavs are a Business Unlike Any Other. Blog Maverick, February 12, 2013. Retrieved from http://blogmaverick.com/2013/02/12/the-nba-is-a-business-unlike-any-other/

Chapter 6: The Investor

The 2008-2009 global financial crisis was unlike anything Mark Cuban had experienced in his professional and entrepreneurial career. Seemingly overnight, the economy tanked. Stocks lost tremendous value. Companies laid off millions. Home values plummeted. Interest rates bottomed.

To lift the nation out of the economic doldrums, government officials debated bailouts and stimulus packages. The key questions included: How much should the government dole out? What types of initiatives would have the best chance of jumpstarting the economy? How much debt could the country afford to tack on in order to lend a helping hand to corporate giants, small business owners, and unemployed workers?

As usual, Cuban had a different approach. He believed entrepreneurs were the key to leading the country out of its economic doldrums. And they didn't need billions in government funds to do it, either. In Cuban's mindset, they just needed a boost to get the momentum going.

So he turned his attention to helping others make their dreams come true. From his Maverick Blog, he announced the Mark Cuban Stimulus Plan. His stimulus plan was specifically designed to "inspire people to create businesses that could quickly become self-funding."

The plan worked like this: People posted their business plans on Cuban's blog. It didn't matter if others stole the idea. In his opinion, if it was good enough to steal, it was needed in as many places around the country as possible.

Cuban committed to investing in some of the ideas, but didn't put any minimum or maximum amounts in place. He did provide readers with a set of rules that would serve as the first hurdle in determining whether an idea received his financial attention. [54]

One of the first rules was that the business could not be advertising supported. As he explained in a follow-up interview, the reason for this strict rule was companies cannot depend on it: "I wanted to invest in companies with tangible products and services that could be sold for a profit. Sales is the lifeblood of any company. If you have a great product or service that is

---

[54] The Mark Cuban Stimulus Plan -- Open Source Funding. Blog Maverick, February 9, 2009. Retrieved from http://blogmaverick.com/2009/02/09/the-mark-cuban-stimulus-plan-open-source-funding/

differentiated and provides value, your entire focus can be on selling it." [55]

The company had to show break-even cash flow within 60 days and a profit within 90 days. Any month a business receiving funding didn't make its numbers, Cuban would turn off the spigot. Another rule was the business owner had to demonstrate that he or she would sell the product or service for more than it cost to produce. Also, the organization must be flat; no middle managers. The business plan had to indicate how much equity Cuban would receive or how he would earn a return on his investment.

"I make no promises that if your business is profitable, that I will invest more money. Once you get the initial funding you are on your own," Cuban wrote in the rules section. "I will make no promises that I will be available to offer help. If I want to, I will. If not, I won't."

Cuban has spent his post-Broadcast.com career serving as one of the country's leading angel investors, a term used to describe affluent individuals who provide capital to start-ups in exchange for an equity position or convertible debt.

---

[55] Bandyk, M. (2009). A New Kind of Stimulus Plan. U.S. News & World Report, 146(6), 75-76.

Helping the up-and-comer is part of his personal brand. He eschews large corporations and believes the best things are built one entrepreneur at a time. And while he's helping entrepreneurs get off the ground, he's collecting as well -- by potentially getting in on the ground floor of the next MicroSolutions or Broadcast.com, and without having to do much of the leg work. If an investment doesn't pan out, he's out a fraction of a percentage of his overall fortune.

As of March 2013, Forbes.com listed Cuban's net worth at $2.4 billion, ranking him 206 on the Forbes 400 list. [56]

Many of Cuban's investments have a technology slant. He has been involved by himself or with an investment group to provide financing recently to the following companies: [57]

- $1 million in a Florida company called LinguaSys, which provides linguistic engineering.

- $1.37 million in debt financing for uBeam, which has created a way to charge up portable electronic devices wirelessly.

---

[56] http://www.forbes.com/profile/mark-cuban/
[57] http://www.crunchbase.com/person/mark-cuban

- $800,000 for vidIQ, billed as the the first YouTube audience development and management suite that helps brands and agencies grow their views and subscribers.

- $1.5 million for Austin, Texas-based Insurance Zebra, a startup that aggregates car insurance quotes the way that Kayak aggregates flight and hotel deals.

- $1.6 million to San Francisco-based Clarity, which connects entrepreneurs with experts, over the phone, for advice on their business challenges.

- $1.85 million for Condition One, which develops next generation immersive video applications and provides an embeddable immersive video player for the iPad, which is licensed to media companies and brands.

- $1.75 million for a company called Upstart, a funding platform and mentoring network that matches students with backers who believe in their potential. Students can receive funding from Upstart to retire student loans, start a business or other uses, then share a percentage of their income with backers over 10 years.

- $1 million for Boston-based Apptopia, a marketplace for brokering mobile app acquisitions.

Mark Cuban's interests go beyond just high-tech. His website, markcubancompanies.com, details all of his various holdings, which include:

- Simple Sugars, an all-natural line of skincare products designed especially for sensitive skin, founded by an 18-year-old.

- The Game Face Company, which has a patented method for applying face paint, makeup and costume masks that makes the product easy to remove.

- KaZam Bikes, which a special bike to help younger children learn how to ride without the use of training wheels.

- Teddy Needs a Bath, a device that helps users clean stuffed animals.

- The Brondell Swash, an advanced toilet seat that provides users with warm water washes, adjustable heated seat, warm air dryer, automatic deodorizer and a wireless remote control.

One can't discuss Cuban's investment philosophy without detailing his most cunning investment decision. Had he not made this move, he likely would never have had the funds to invest in this stable of startups, and he certainly would not have enough to buy a basketball team or any other sports franchise.

When Yahoo! purchased Broadcast.com for $5 billion in April 1999, it paid for the transaction in Yahoo! stock, which at the time of the close of the sale was worth $145 a share. At its peak, the company was trading around $500 a share. However, part of the deal was that Cuban could not sell his shares for six months. Fearing that the company was overvalued and could quickly lose value -- costing him a fortune -- Cuban hedged his Yahoo! stock.

The hedge strategy Cuban used was a risk-reversal, which consists of selling a call and buying a put option. It's a complicated financial transaction, but it essentially protects against unfavorable, downward price movements. The downside is that it also limits how much profit you can earn when the stock price goes higher.

Call options gives you the right to buy a stock from the investor who sold you the option at a specific price on or before a specific date. For example, if you have a $35 call option on a stock and it rises about that mark before the option expires, you can pay $35 a share and essentially get discounted stock.

A put option works the opposite. You have right to sell a stock to an investor who sold you the option at a specific price on or before a specified date. So if you have a $25 put option and the stock falls below that mark, you can sell your shares for more than they're currently worth.

Though it cost Cuban $20 million up front to hedge his Yahoo! shares, the alternative would have been far worse. By the time he would have been able to sell the stock outright, according to the buyout agreement, the value of his holdings would have plummeted about 90 percent. The Mark Cuban story would have turned out much differently. [58]

The bottom line on this complicated transaction is that Cuban understood the risk of holding onto Yahoo! stock when it appeared likely to him that its value could dive. He didn't want to lose the fortune because of the whims of the market. He was more than willing to surrender a few million to hold onto his billions. He guessed right, and it wouldn't be the last time.

To Cuban, there's a huge difference between spending money and losing it. He has no problem handing out large tips, spending lavishly on clothes and cars and buying whatever he desires. That's the

---

[58] Leonard, D. (2007). MARK CUBAN MAY BE A BILLIONAIRE, BUT WHAT HE REALLY NEEDS IS RESPECT. Fortune, 156(8), 172-182.

beauty of being rich. What he can't stand is losing it and having nothing to show for the loss. That's why he's particularly selective about the types of investments he enters, and why he's so suspicious of the stock market.

For example, a business associate approached him in 2004 about investing in a hedge fund consisting of Private Investment in Public Equity (PIPE) funds. PIPEs invest directly into a public company through private deals in order to acquire stock at a discount. Companies, mostly small and medium-sized businesses, issue PIPE funds to raise needed capital. Cuban said no to this associate several times. In addition, he got out of any company that did PIPE deals.

Cuban turned out to be rightfully skittish. When the financial crisis struck in 2008, hedge funds couldn't get out of illiquid positions in microcap companies and they all crashed. [59]

Though he avoided investing in the offering, the pitch ended up nearly getting Cuban in trouble. In 2008, he was charged by the Securities and Exchange Commission with insider trading.

---

[59] How I Helped Mark Cuban Make a Billion Dollars and 5 Things I Learned from Him. The Altucher Confidential. Retrieved from http://www.jamesaltucher.com/2011/04/why-im-jealous-of-mark-cuban-and-5-things-i-learned-from-him/

According to the SEC's charges, Cuban sold 600,000 shares of a company called Mamma.com, a meta-search engine. The commission accused Cuban of selling the stock after learning of the company's PIPE offering through the aforementioned business associate. Rather than suffer dilution, the SEC claimed, Cuban sold the stock before the PIPE offering, saving himself $750,000. The case was eventually dismissed by a federal judge. [60]

Contrary to his sometimes buffoonish persona, Cuban is an extraordinary well-informed and insightful businessman. And like his philosophy on entrepreneurship, his concepts for fixing what he believes need repair are unique and often universally rejected by the powers-that-be.

For example, he has crusaded against certain stock market manipulations for some time:

> "Investors should be rewarded for actually owning companies and gaining returns on their investments. Financial engineers should have to pay a premium for the risk they introduce to the entire financial system. It was

---

[60] Schachter, K. (2008). UPDATE: Mark Cuban Charged With Insider Trading. Red Herring, 10.

92

not investors that brought on the last two crashes. It was the financial engineers.

The beautiful thing about this country is that we like to work hard, and we like to take chances. Unfortunately, over the last 15 years, the incentives have been to take chances as a financial engineer rather than as an entrepreneur. We give far more money to people who play games with financial instruments than we give to people who come up with ideas for the next big thing. That needs to change if we want to remain a leader in this world." [61]

During an appearance at his alma mater, Cuban told students gathered to hear him speak at Assembly Hall that the best thing they could invest in was themselves. When asked later to clarify that statement, Cuban responded:

"They wanted a stock tip. I told them that the dumbest thing they could do now is buy stock. There are no shortcuts to making money. The stock market is so big, and there

---

[61] Entrepreneurs, Investors and Financial Engineers -- Not All are "Business People." Blog Maverick, October 17, 2012. Retrieved from http://blogmaverick.com/2012/10/17/entrepreneurs-investors-and-financial-engineers-not-all-are-businesspeople/

are so many people involved in it, you have to get an intelligent advantage to make any money. It takes a lot of years of trial and error to get rich in the stock market. I told them to invest in sweat equity, to invest in themselves. Invest in equity that they understand and know better than anybody." [62]

Cuban is the type of person who doesn't stop at identifying a problem. He offers solutions. And in true Cuban fashion, they're quite different from the solutions proposed by the status quo.

To solve the problem of financial engineering and get people back to investing, Cuban proposes that there be no taxes on any gains from the sale of stock or bonds purchased, nor from dividends and interest, during an IPO and held for five years or more. He would not allow the stock to be borrowed against. Investors who sell during this five-year window would be taxed at their personal regular income tax rate. [63]

---

[62] 20 Questions for Mark Cuban. Magbloom.com, February/March 2008. Retrieved from http://www.magbloom.com/wp-content/uploads/2012/02/20Q_bloom10.pdf

[63] Entrepreneurs, Investors and Financial Engineers -- Not All are "Business People." Blog Maverick, October 17, 2012. Retrieved from http://blogmaverick.com/2012/10/17/entrepreneurs-investors-and-financial-engineers-not-all-are-businesspeople/

Cuban also once introduced the idea of hedge fund that placed sports bets instead of investing in stocks or bonds. The idea seemed to germinate less from an appreciation for sports gambling and more from his disdain of the public investment markets.

> "Unlike the stock market, you know the rules exactly. You know without question, the house is going to play by the rules. The gaming commission appears to actually enforce rules of play, unlike the SEC. And then there are sports bets. Like any other investment or bet, the question always come down to whether there is good information available, who knows how to use it better, and who is the competition and are they smart or not." [64]

Cuban never pursued the idea, largely due to an NBA prohibition on league representatives being involved in gambling. But another group did. In 2010, a London-based investment company named Centaur launched a hedge fund called Galileo. The fund's managers analyzed and traded the betting markets. [65]

---

[64] My New Hedge Fund. Blog Maverick, November 27, 2004. Retrieved from http://blogmaverick.com/2004/11/27/my-new-hedge-fund/

[65] Sports Betting Hedge Fund Becomes Reality. CNBC.com, April 7, 2010. Retrieved from http://www.cnbc.com/id/36218041

However, it only lasted a few years before going out of business for unspecified reasons. [66]

Despite his penchant for investing in the next big thing, Cuban also once expressed interest in getting into one of the oldest businesses: newspapers.

"Newspapers are a perfect example of how economics dominate common sense. Contrary to popular belief, newspapers aren't dying. Newspapers are making tons of money; they just aren't keeping their shareholders happy, they aren't meeting the expectations on Wall Street. The problem with newspapers is that they're trying to grow like they're Internet companies in 1999. Their shareholders are bitching at them about not showing growth in share prices. The minute you have to run your business for share prices, you've lost." [67]

Being a billionaire affords him the kind of freedom to chase what everybody else thinks is a lost cause. He doesn't have to take risks anymore. He doesn't need

---

[66] Sports Betting Hedge Fund Closes. ESPN.com, January 31, 2012. Retrieved from http://espn.go.com/blog/truehoop/post/_/id/36339/sports-betting-hedge-fund-closes

[67] What I've Learned: Mark Cuban. Esquire.com, November 17, 2008. Retrieved from http://www.esquire.com/features/what-ive-learned/ESQ1206BBCUBAN_182_1

the big score. He can spend on things he wants, and invest the rest conservatively, and the money will always be there. If he dumps a bunch of money into something like HDNet and never earns it all back, at least he spent it on something he enjoyed. And there's plenty more where that came from.

He's also free from the institutions he believes have the wrong motives. He will probably never take any of his companies public and put himself at the mercy of shareholders and directors watching over his shoulder.

> "If I'm making money, I'm happy. If we are profitable, great. If I make more than last year, great! It isn't like, 'Dang, I've got to grow 15 percent this year.' If I'm making money, if I'm paying my bills, I'm happy. Save a little bit, all the better. What's fucked up is, the people who run public companies don't think this way. They're just trying to get rich. The idea of running a public company isn't 'Wow, I can run a company.' It's 'Wow, I might be able to get rich!' Not just a-couple-million-dollars rich, but a-couple-million-dollars-a-year, fuck-you-money rich." [68]

---

[68] What I've Learned: Mark Cuban. Esquire.com, November 17, 2008. Retrieved from http://www.esquire.com/features/what-ive-learned/ESQ1206BBCUBAN_182_1

And by choosing not to chain himself to the public markets, Cuban doesn't have to behave himself for the sake of a stodgy board of directors and institutional investors. He can be himself at all times.

Chapter 7: The Celebrity

Mark Cuban originally retired at the age of 31, after selling MicroSolutions. He was a young multimillionaire who wanted to have fun.

So, of course, he landed in Hollywood.

Manhattan Beach, to be more specific. He spent $125,000 on a lifetime pass to fly anywhere on American Airlines, which he used to visit 11 countries. He bought a house on a whim. He partied, fornicated, and hung out at the beach. He also took acting classes and appeared in two movies in the mid 1990s. [69]

If you look them up on IMDB, you will find very little details on either, not even a plot synopsis. The first movie, released in 1994, was *Talking About Sex* starring Kim Wayans, sister of Keenen Ivory, Damon, Marlon and the rest of the Wayans comedy family. Cuban played a character named "Macho Mark."

---

[69] The Billionaire. Esquire.com, April 1, 2000. Retrieved from http://www.esquire.com/features/billionaire-cuban-sound-0400

In 1995, he appeared in a movie called *Lost at Sea*, a 90-minute R-rated action movie. The IMDB page for this flick lists five total cast members. The lead actor was Steve Sayre, whose biggest Hollywood credit is as the fight choreographer for the original Rocky. Cuban is listed in the film credits as "Villain." No other details about the movie are listed.

Since becoming a famous entrepreneur, sports team owner and billionaire, his occasional movie roles have still skewed to the obscure. He played a character named Seamus in the 2008 raunchy comedy, *One, Two, Many*, a $500,000 budget film about a guy trying to find a girlfriend who's OK with threesomes. He also had bit roles in the straight-to-video film *Like Mike 2: Streetball* (2002), and a cameo in *Tim and Eric's Billion Dollar Movie* (2012), which grossed a total of $201,000 at the box office.

The latter film was produced by 2929 Productions, Cuban's film company. The movie is a bizarre satire about two guys who get $1 billion to make a movie, only they squander most of the loot before they have a complete film made. In order to make the money back, they attempt to revitalize a shopping mall in decline.

One can hardly imagine other billionaires taking time out of their busy schedules to act in a raunchy sex comedy. Then again, he may be the only billionaire in the world who would provide commentary on his college debauchery, rather than try to hide it.

That's what happened when Deadspin.com discovered a photo gallery of his rugby playing exploits at Indiana on his Google+ profile. The site's editors asked him for permission to link the gallery. Not only did Cuban oblige, he wrote descriptions for those he could remember. [70]

One photo showed Cuban's friends being slid naked on a table toward a pyramid of cups, which Cuban called "rugger bowling." Another depicted Cuban laying on top of a woman with his rear end in her face, and another licking the face of a woman standing next to a friend. There was also one that captured what Cuban called the Indiana University 'elephant walk,' a ritual whereby naked men on their knees moved in a train formation. Cuban was not one of the participants in that photo.

These aren't the kinds of photos your average billionaire would be proud to show off. But then again, there is only one man that's almost universally considered to be "the coolest billionaire."

[70] "Hey, It Was The Seventies": Mark Cuban Narrates A Gallery Of His Debaucherous College Rugby Years. Deadspin.com, July 7, 2011. Retrieved from http://deadspin.com/5818693/hey-it-was-the-seventies-mark-cuban-narrates-a-gallery-of-his-debaucherous-college-rugby-years/

Mark Cuban loves the spotlight. He made five appearances, playing a fictionalized version of himself on the hit HBO show *Entourage* and played the role of Mark Smith in a two-part episode of the Chuck Norris drama *Walker, Texas Ranger* in 2000. He has appeared on *Real Time with Bill Maher*, *The Colbert Report*, *The Tonight Show*, and countless other talk and late night shows. He played himself in the updated TV series *Dallas*, a 2008 episode of the animated classic *The Simpsons*, and made a cameo on the HBO sports comedy *Arli$$*.

In December of 2007, Cuban guest hosted World Wrestling Entertainment's popular weekly television show, *Monday Night Raw*. He told wrestler Randy Orton that the only reason he won a wrestling match is because "these WWE refs are worse than NBA refs." Later in the evening, he got caught in a 'melee' between wrestlers and was thrown through a wooden table.

In 2010, the NBA All-Star Game was played in Dallas, and the hometown billionaire found a way to become the center of attention, yet again. He competed in the Celebrity All-Star Game, and one of his most memorable moments from the event was when Cuban had a shot rejected by actor Chris Tucker.

It's all part of the Cuban persona to want to be in front of the camera, even if just for a scene. That's why, even as a sports owner, he's better known than his players. And whereas most angel investors like to stay in the background, Cuban does much of his current investing in front of a national television audience as a panelist on ABC's *Shark Tank*.

In 2007, Cuban competed on *Dancing with the Stars*. Why would a billionaire who just had hip replacement surgery compete on a show reserved for has-been celebrities and retired athletes? "Because I can," Cuban wrote in his blog. Of course, he elaborates, offering even more insight into what make him tick:

> "It actually is more surprising to me that some people would even think twice if asked to participate on the show. I'm the first to admit that I'm the luckiest guy in the world. I can honestly say I wake up every morning with a smile knowing what a wonderful family, friends and life I have. It's the exact same way I felt when I was broke.
>
> Money makes so many things in life easier, but it can't buy you a positive outlook on life. Fortunately, how any of us approaches each of our days is completely up to us. It's not something you can buy or sell. It's not hard to

put a smile on your face every day, but for some reason some people find it impossible to do. Not me.

The opportunity to do something unique that makes me smile is something I try not to pass up. Dancing with the Stars is just that. It's not about how well I can dance. It's about the opportunity to compete at something I enjoy. It's about doing something that makes me smile every minute I'm doing it or even thinking about it. [71]

One interesting footnote to that appearance occurred five years later. He admitted in a radio interview that he was trying to work out a trade for Kobe Bryant during the rehearsals.[72]

Nowadays, Cuban is a regular on the ABC reality hit, *Shark Tank*. The show, which premiered in 2009, is a natural for Cuban, as it features business pitches from aspiring entrepreneurs to a panel of potential

---

[71] Dancing with the Stars and the Meaning of Life. Blog Maverick, September 7, 2007. Retrieved from http://blogmaverick.com/2007/09/07/dancing-with-the-stars-and-the-meaning-of-life/

[72] While on 'Dancing with the Stars' Mark Cuban Almost Traded for Kobe Bryant. CBSSports.com, August 22, 2012. Retrieved from http://www.cbssports.com/nba/blog/eye-on-basketball/19867305/while-on-dancing-with-the-stars-mark-cuban-almost-traded-for-kobe-bryant-

investors. Cuban became a panelist for a few episodes in season 2, then was inserted as a full-time cast member in season 3.

The show received a nomination for a Producers Guild Award in 2013. In 2012, *Shark Tank* received an Emmy nomination for Outstanding Reality Program and a nomination for a Critics' Choice Television Award for Best Reality Series.

In addition to Cuban, business owners looking for seed money also face real estate mogul Barbara Corcoran; "Queen of QVC" Lori Greiner; technology innovator Robert Herjavec; fashion and branding expert Daymond John; and venture capitalist Kevin O'Leary.

The panel has heard pitches on everything from beer-infused ice cream to pre-packaged meals for pets, a rent-a-grandma business, a fragrance that smells like money, and a spring-loaded laundry hamper, just to name a few.

> "Shark Tank is not scripted at all. When the entrepreneur walks into the shark tank the ONLY thing we know is their first name. NOTHING else.
>
> The only "scripted" part of the show is this... the producers tell us before every show... 'if an

entrepreneur looks like they are going to cry, shut up and let them.' They love tears. That's the only scripting.

We get the chance to do due diligence after the show. As a result, you uncover things that were not brought up in the show, so it's not unusual for a deal to fall through in the DD phase. I have had things like people who never paid their taxes, people who lied on the show, and people who didn't think that if they spent money on their personal credit cards it should be considered an expense. You name it.

There is so much pressure on the entrepreneur during the show that sometimes they say what they think we want to hear rather than the truth." [73]

In addition to being on a hit TV program, Cuban is also helping entrepreneurs through *Shark Tank*. Just for appearing on the show, contestants have to agree to give up a 5% equity stake or 2% of all future royalties to the producers. But several who have been on the program said it was worth it.

---

[73] Mark Cuban: What Entrepreneurs Need to Know Before Starting a Business. Entrepreneur.com, December 26, 2012. Retrieved from http://www.entrepreneur.com/blog/225357

Derek Pacque, a 24 year-old CEO who appeared on the show, told *Forbes* that his appearance had a major impact on his business. He founded CoatChex, a company that's developed a portable, automated system for checking coats and bags at events. He turned down an equity investment from Cuban when he appeared on the show. But after the episode aired, the company website received 1,000 hits per second. What's more, the company landed deals with American Express, NBC and Mercedes Benz, and it raised $200,000 in angel funding at better terms than what he was offered by the Sharks.

Likewise, 31-year-old Phil Dumas said the program helped him close a deal with a company he had long been in talks with. Dumas is the founder of UniKey, which has developed technology to connect smartphones with door locks. [74]

"I try to quickly decide if I'm investing in the business or the person," said Cuban. "From there I can determine whether I want to own the business, or

---

[74] Is 'Shark Tank' Really Worth 5% of Your Company? Business Owners Say 'Absolutely.' Forbes.com, June 13, 2013. Retrieved from http://www.forbes.com/sites/jjcolao/2013/06/13/is-shark-tank-really-worth-5-of-your-company-business-owners-say-absolutely/

whether it's an inexpensive way to hire someone smart to run the business." [75]

Not all of Cuban's reality TV efforts have been hits. In 2004, he launched *The Benefactor*. The premise was 16 contestants competed to win $1 million from Cuban based on his assessment of their skills during weekly tasks. The show never found an audience, despite being the lead-in to Monday Night Football, and was cancelled after just one month on the air.

A quote attributed to Cuban illuminates, perhaps, the root of his need for attention. Back in 1997, a company called Reset was getting in the business of live streaming of TV shows. AudioNet contacted the company because it wanted Reset to use its technology to do the live streaming. A salesperson pleading his case to the executives at Reset said: "Mark Cuban wants to go public and we NEED press releases. Press releases drive IPOs. This would be a great press release." [76]

---

[75] Mark Cuban, Billionaire (Scared, Broke and Jobless). Subvert Magazine, September 10, 2012. Retrieved from http://www.subvertmagazine.com/blog/mark-cuban/

[76] How I Helped Mark Cuban Make a Billion Dollars and 5 Things I Learned from Him. The Altucher Confidential. Retrieved from http://www.jamesaltucher.com/2011/04/why-im-jealous-of-mark-cuban-and-5-things-i-learned-from-him/

Companies need publicity. Brands need publicity. Any kind of publicity. Any kind of attention. All of Cuban's major holdings, from the Mavericks to 2929 Productions to AXS TV owe much of their success to the Mark Cuban brand and the ideas that brand generates.

The Mark Cuban brand needs to stay in the public eye. It needs to forge and reinforce a certain reputation. It needs to reach a certain audience and create buzz. Because without a strong and viable Mark Cuban brand, the companies he owns and pumps money into likely wouldn't continue to thrive. At least not in the way they have.

Magic? The golden touch? Whatever "it" is, Mark Cuban has it!

Chapter 8: The King

The title of this final chapter doesn't mean to imply that Mark Cuban is royalty. In fact, his anti-establishment ways would shun any comparison to nobility. And it isn't because he's one of the richest men in the world. Instead, the title 'king' summarizes, in one word, the life of Mark Cuban, who always has and always will be the king of his world, his destiny and his life.

If you had to summarize the life of Mark Cuban, one way would be to divide it in thirds.

The first third encompasses the early struggles. He grew up in a middle class family in Pittsburgh. His father, Norton, worked as an automobile upholsterer. Mark was your run-of-the-mill Jewish kid, not a genius but not a slacker either; not popular but not a bullied nerd. He never wanted for basic needs, never experienced poverty, but lived a life when a meal at restaurant was a special occasion. It wasn't a bad life, but it was far less than he desired for his adulthood. He used to drive through ritzy neighborhoods admiring the stately houses, telling himself that the people living in those castles worked hard to get there. If they could do it, he told himself over and over, so could he.

He was lured to Dallas from a stable job in Indiana. He had nothing with him when he drove a 1977 Fiat X19 with a hole in the floorboard and leaking oil to the heart of the Lone Star State. He arrived in the city of J.R. Ewing and the Dallas Cowboys with dreams as big as Texas.

He moved into a tiny three-bedroom apartment with five friends struggling to make a living. He had no bedroom, not even a bed to sleep on or a closet or dresser to store what few clothes he brought. He drank from $12 bottles of champagne while he tended bar, waiting for his big break.

"I never thought of packing it up and moving home. Not one single time," said Cuban. "I just knew I had to figure it out. The only person I would depend on was me. I wasn't always optimistic. There were times when I got scared. I was broke. I had no job. But I kept on pushing. I wasn't going to quit. After all I had nothing to lose. All I had was what I had and it wasn't much." [77]

---

[77] Mark Cuban, Billionaire (Scared, Broke and Jobless). Subvert Magazine, September 10, 2012. Retrieved from http://www.subvertmagazine.com/blog/mark-cuban/

SEAN HUFF

The middle third is when he made his first million and then first billion by doing all the things he espouses to others. He went after his dreams. He worked hard. He pursued his passions. And he cashed in not once, but twice -- building valuable properties in MicroSolutions and Broadcast.com.

When a blogger tried to make the case that Cuban is not a visionary, but just lucky, he responded:

> "Yeah Im lucky. And proud to be. I was lucky with MicroSolutions when we started selling LANs in 1983 before anyone else and sold to Compuserve. I was lucky selling corporate business applications I wrote and developed. I was lucky with Precept, a hedge fund built on my tech background that I sold (didn't know about that one did you.). I was lucky with Broadcast.com, I was lucky to start HDNet years before anyone else thought HD had a chance, lucky with about 10 other companies, too. [78]

The last third may best be described as the evolution of the Mark Cuban brand. In the world of marketing, all brands evolve over time. Those that can't change with the rapid pace of innovation and advancement eventually cease to exist. Cuban has adjusted his brand to account for his older age, his relatively new responsibilities as husband and father of three, and the changing world around him.

> "I mean, I don't think I'm all that different than before. Money doesn't show up in how I dress. It doesn't show up in what I do or where I go or how I act. It just makes life simpler. I was happy when I was broke and I'm happy now.
>
> What defines me is nothing I ever think about. It's not like, what's my legacy going to be, or how do people think about me, or don't they know this about me or that about me. I don't pay attention to that at all. If anything defines me it's how my kids turn out. That's the only important job I have." [79]

Cuban is much different on the outside in this third act of his life than he was in the first two. He's made a fortune, become famous, and won an NBA championship. The now 54-year-old has a net worth of $2.4 billion as of March 2013, which ranks him

---

[79] 20 Questions for Mark Cuban. Magbloom.com, February/March 2008. Retrieved from http://www.magbloom.com/wp-content/uploads/2012/02/20Q_bloom10.pdf

613th on Forbes list of the world's billionaires, 213th in the United States. Anything more he would accomplish from this day forward would be gravy on top of an already remarkable life.

Does Mark Cuban still have the drive and determination that he did before? In some ways yes, in others, no.

Early on in this third stage, Cuban continued to do everything he could on a grand scale. He hired John Mellencamp to entertain guests at a barbeque shortly after he cashed out on the Broadcast.com deal. When he married longtime girlfriend Tiffany in 2002, the bachelor party guests were flown from three different cities in Cuban's private plane, supplied with alcohol and female dancers, to Las Vegas. The couple's wedding reception took place in American Airlines Arena, with rock legend Sammy Hagar providing the entertainment.

> "The best thing about the money, I guess, is that I don't have to prove myself anymore. There are some guys you talk to, they want to move up the list. They're like, I'm shooting for the top twenty, the top ten, whatever. I don't need to move up the fuckin' list. I'm the first to realize that my success is yesterday's news. But I'm not necessarily concerned about thinking, 'Can I do it again?' What's more

important to me is: Can I find something new that consumes me, that entertains me to the same extent, that challenges me in the same way? It's the never-ending question, I guess." [80]

Wealth may have changed Cuban on the outside, but it did little to alter his heart and motivations. He still eats roast beef sandwiches, likes to go to movies, and worries about his weight like any other middle aged man. He remains loyal to the friends he partied with at Indiana University and crashed with in his first Dallas apartment.

Mark Cuban lives like a king because he can essentially do what he wants, the laws of his state and country notwithstanding. He has the money to do anything, go anywhere or buy whatever his heart desires. He has maintained independence from the institutions that want their billionaire CEOs to act in a dignified manner. And since he has no interest in ever running for public office, there's no harm in sharing tasteless college photographs with the world.

He competed on *Dancing with the Stars* not because he had to, but because he could. He shared the

---

[80] The Billionaire. Esquire.com, April 1, 2000. Retrieved from http://www.esquire.com/features/billionaire-cuban-sound-0400

proceeds of the sale of Broadcast.com with its employees not because he had to, but because he could. He spent a day working at a Dairy Queen not because he had to, but because he could. Few people in his position could get away with hanging out in a bar with college students a few days before the Super Bowl, but Mark Cuban can.

"I mean, some people can run to freedom," Cuban says. "I can sell to freedom. And that's what I learned when I was a kid. Time and freedom. Those are the ultimate assets, absolutely. My self-fulfillment doesn't come from the money. It comes from just knowing that intellectually there are no bounds--that's the number-one thing. Nobody telling me what to do. Just me doing things because I can." [81]

Another thing he can do with his wealth and fame is help others. Whether it's the natural progression of a maturing man, the result of having a family of his own, some atonement of past sins or simply because he has the means, Mark Cuban is spending a lot of money simply helping others. And not all of it is in the traditional charitable sense. The irony is that he virtually built his fortune on his own, save for the investments of his various business partners.

---

[81] The Billionaire. Esquire.com, April 1, 2000. Retrieved from http://www.esquire.com/features/billionaire-cuban-sound-0400

For example, in February 2013, Cuban announced that he wanted a new uniform for the Mavericks from the 2015-16 season. But he wasn't hiring a professional design or branding firm to draw the new threads. He solicited all comers through his blog to submit design ideas. If he found one he liked, he would use it. As with many of his offers to help up-and-comers, Cuban made no promises that any of the submitted ideas would be used. [82]

That initiative fits with one part of the Mark Cuban brand that will always stay constant: his belief that the best ideas come from individuals, not companies.

He has also used his popular blog to encourage men to their colons examined, and he did it in typical Mark Cuban fashion.

> "I'm getting to that age where it pays to be proactive and start getting tested for the myriad of things that can go wrong with my body. One of the things I wanted to get over with is a check for colon cancer. Although I'm officially younger than the 'suggested age' for a colonoscopy, I wanted to get it out of the

---

[82] Help the Mavs Design Our Next Uniform! Blog Maverick, May 13, 2013. Retrieved from http://blogmaverick.com/2013/05/13/help-the-mavs-design-our-next-uniform/

way. I had read and heard too many stories about people who found polyps and how if they had only caught them a little sooner it would be no big deal to remove them. So I set my appointment and went for it."

"I was definitely nervous. Despite doctors and nurses telling me it would be a breeze, I was naturally skeptical. A breeze was an overstatement. I can honestly say that if it made medical sense to get one done every year, I would have no problem with it. It was easy and breezy.

Once I got into the Gastro Room where they did these, they told me that they were going to knock me out, and I would get a nap and wake up like nothing happened. They were right. One minute I'm talking rugby, the next I'm waking up, picking up the conversation where I left off and being told to 'dispell the air in my system.'

No where else can you rip off some huge farts and have 3 nurses and a doctor, while maintaining a very professional demeanor, tell you that you aren't done yet and demand that you let loose a few more. Then it was up to get dressed and out the door so my wife could give me a ride home."

"Bottom line is that your life just might depend on getting tested for colon cancer. There is absolutely nothing to be afraid of. It's truly easy and breezy. Do it." [83]

In addition to his investment in startups and his investments in investigative journalism, Cuban has also become a philanthropist. Shortly after the Iraq War started, Cuban created the Fallen Patriot Fund to help families of killed or wounded soldiers. The fund has provided $2.6 million to families of soldiers.

"I don't think I've ever taken it for granted that anything I've accomplished is all because my grandparents, my parents, our friends have fought. And kids today are out there fighting to make sure all of us here have that opportunity. Before every game during the national anthem, I say to myself 'thank you' to everybody who fought before and everyone fighting now to keep this country so great. And when we invaded Iraq I was finally in a position to put my money where my mouth was. We started the Fallen Patriot Fund so I could at least try to help.

---

[83] My Colonoscopy. Blog Maverick, June 14, 2007. Retrieved from http://blogmaverick.com/2011/09/10/my-colonoscopy-2/

Actually, the Fallen Patriot Fund is the only one of my foundations that I've publicly put my name on. For me to give money to anybody else, one of the requirements is that you have to be anonymous, because I don't ever want to think I'm giving money to get PR. I want to always make sure I'm doing it because that's the reason I want to do it. I'll promote the Fallen Patriot Fund, but even then, you don't see me going out there and talking about it a lot. It stands on its own. We've been able to raise enough and I've contributed enough that we've been able to cover expenses. And if we were ever to run short, then I'd put up my own money. That's the way it works." [84]

A key difference between the Cuban of old and the older Cuban is how thinly he's spread compared to his early years.

He focused all of his efforts on MicroSolutions and then on Broadcast.com. Now he has a sports team, a TV network, motion picture business, a chain of movie theaters, a production company, TV

---

[84] 20 Questions for Mark Cuban. Magbloom.com, February/March 2008. Retrieved from http://www.magbloom.com/wp-content/uploads/2012/02/20Q_bloom10.pdf

appearances, and a slew of other companies in his investment portfolio.

Without Cuban's 100 percent focus, do any of them have a chance to become the next big thing?

Certainly, fortunes don't grow as fast as they used to. Much of the rest of the world has caught up to Cuban's methods. There are more ideas, but less money.

While he does acknowledge that he lacks the time to add much else to his portfolio, he has expressed some interest in trying to turn around the newspaper industry, which follows the rule of doing something that nobody else wants to be part of. Perhaps Amazon founder Jeff Bezos' recent decision to acquire *The Washington Post* will tempt Cuban to get into the game.

Another sign the world of Mark Cuban is different: He used one of his blog posts to explain a joke he made on a podcast with ESPN's popular sports columnist, Bill Simmons, aka "The Sports Guy." Simmons and Cuban were debating the merits of the "The Kiss Cam," a staple at most sporting events in which a camera will fixate on a couple, who are then supposed to kiss while the rest of the stadium or arena watches. Simmons said he loved "Kiss Cam," to which Cuban replied, "That's because you and your boyfriend are always on it."

> "I made a mistake in making the comment. I wasn't trying to be hurtful. It wasn't a comment on anyone's sexuality. It was just me trying to be funny. It wasn't. I quickly realized it and tried to fix it. I hoped at the time I didn't offend anyone.

> This blog post is not about trying to defend what I said. I'm not trying to defend my sense of humor. I'm not trying to convince you I'm not a homophobe. I'm not trying to justify anything at all.

> I guess what I am doing is admitting that at some level I am prejudiced and that I recognize that I am. There are a lot of things in my life that I need to improve at. This is one of them. Sometimes I make stupid throw away comments that I quickly realize are wrong. It doesn't happen often, but it happens. It was a mistake and I realized it. I learned from it.

> I'm the last to be politically correct and the last thing I am trying to be here is politically correct. I honestly don't give a shit what you think about me. But I think being the person

I want to be includes not blurting out throw away jokes about sexuality, race, ethnicity, size, disability or other things people have no say in about themselves. I'm the guy who still feels bad about punching Michael Cooper in the stomach in 6th grade purely because he was overweight, even though I made the point to apologize to him when I ran into him at a reunion years later.

Even if I don't care about you, it doesn't mean I'm ok with making you uncomfortable or upset with a comment that references anything that is out of your control. That is not the person I want to be.

I'm happy to pick on you if you root for the wrong team. I'm happy to pick on you if you like doing The Wave. I'm happy to pick on you for a lot of reasons. Your sexuality should never be one of those reasons.

I like who I am. I love my life. But that doesn't mean I won't always try to be a better version of me. And yes, I feel better having written this blog post." [85]

---

[85] Am I a Homophobe? Blog Maverick, March 9, 2012. Retrieved from http://blogmaverick.com/2012/03/09/am-i-a-homophobe/

But unlike other celebrities' brands that have crumbled because of saying the wrong thing with a camera or recorder going, Mark Cuban's brand has survived and continued to thrive. That may be because his brand is grounded in the ideals of the common American: Cheer for the underdog, give the person willing to work hard a fair shot, and run a business for the benefit of you and your customers, not shareholders and governments.

He's not trying to impress stuffed shirt executives or conservative investors. He's reaching out to people like him: people with dreams, people with energy, people with creativity, people with determination and people with no fear.

A reader of his blogs and the hundreds of articles written about him would be hard pressed to find any mention of a professional mentor. There seems not to exist a person that a young Mark Cuban looked up to, nobody who can take even partial credit for molding him, teaching him the ways of business or helping him learn from his own mistakes. There is plenty of mention of the bosses who pushed him into entrepreneurship because of what Cuban believed was their incompetence as managers.

In all of Cuban's interviews, blog posts and book excerpts, one quote seems to encapsulate everything in this book and everything about the way Mark Cuban has lived his life to this point. It's the concluding sentence to a blog post he wrote in 2007 titled "Dancing with the Stars and the Meaning of Life."

"When I'm 90 years old and talking to my grandkids and hopefully great-grand kids, I won't be the grandparent who tells them about the things I wished I had done and how they should experience life, I will be the grandparent with tons of great stories that hopefully inspires them to live their lives to the fullest." [86]

---

[86] Dancing with the Stars and the Meaning of Life. Blog Maverick, September 7, 2007. Retrieved from http://blogmaverick.com/2007/09/07/dancing-with-the-stars-and-the-meaning-of-life/